RENAISSANCE

VOLUME 4

Eyck — Government

GROLIER
EDUCATIONAL

Published by Grolier Educational
Sherman Turnpike
Danbury, Connecticut 06816

Set ISBN 0-7172-5673-1
Volume 4 ISBN 0-7172-5666-9

Library of Congress Cataloging-in-Publication Data

Renaissance.
    p. cm.
Summary: Chronicles the cultural and artistic flowering
known as the Renaissance that flourished in Europe and
in other parts of the world from approximately 1375 to
1575 A.D.
Includes index.
Contents: v. 1. Africa–Bologna — v. 2. Books and libraries–
Constantinople — v. 3. Copernicus–Exploration — v. 4.
Eyck–Government — v. 5. Guilds and crafts–Landscape
painting — v. 6. Language–Merchants — v. 7. Michelangelo–
Palaces and villas — v. 8. Palestrina–Reformation — v. 9.
Religious dissent–Tapestry — v. 10. Technology–Zwingli.
  ISBN 0-7172-5673-1 (set : alk. paper)
  1. Renaissance—Juvenile literature. [1. Renaissance.]
  I. Grolier Educational (Firm)
  CB361 .R367 2002
  940.2'1—dc21
                                    2002002477

For information address the publisher:
Grolier Educational, Sherman Turnpike,
Danbury, Connecticut 06816

FOR BROWN PARTWORKS

Project Editor:	Shona Grimbly
Deputy Editor:	Rachel Bean
Text Editor:	Chris King
Designer:	Sarah Williams
Picture Research:	Veneta Bullen
Maps:	Colin Woodman
Design Manager:	Lynne Ross
Production:	Matt Weyland
Managing Editor:	Tim Cooke
Consultant:	Stephen A. McKnight
	University of Florida

Printed and bound in Singapore

ABOUT THIS BOOK

This is one of a set of 10 books that tells the story of the Renaissance—a time of discovery and change in the world. It was during this period—roughly from 1375 to 1575—that adventurous mariners from Europe sailed the vast oceans in tiny ships and found the Americas and new sea routes to the Spice Islands of the East. The influx of gold and silver from the New World and the increase in trade made many merchants and traders in Europe extremely rich. They spent some of their wealth on luxury goods like paintings and gold and silver items for their homes, and this created a new demand for the work of artists of all kinds. Europe experienced a cultural flowering as great artists like Leonardo da Vinci, Michelangelo, and Raphael produced masterpieces that have never been surpassed.

At the same time, scholars were rediscovering the works of the ancient Greek and Roman writers, and this led to a new way of looking at the world based on observation and the importance of the individual. This humanism, together with other new ideas, spread more rapidly than ever before thanks to the development of printing with movable type.

There was upheaval in the church too. Thinkers such as Erasmus and Luther began to question the teachings of the established church, and this eventually led to a breakaway from the Catholic church and the setting up of Protestant churches—an event called the Reformation.

The set focuses on Europe, but it also looks at how societies in other parts of the world such as Africa, China, India, and the Americas were developing, and the ways in which the Islamic and Christian worlds interacted.

The entries in this set are arranged alphabetically and are illustrated with paintings, photographs, drawings, and maps, many from the Renaissance period. Each entry ends with a list of cross-references to other entries in the set, and at the end of each book there is a timeline to help you relate events to one another in time.

There is also a useful "Further Reading" list that includes websites, a glossary of special terms, and an index covering the whole set.

Contents

VOLUME 4

Eyck, Jan van

Jan van Eyck (about 1385–1441) was one of the most important northern European artists of the 15th century. He introduced a sparkling realism, or lifelike style, to painting based on his meticulous observation of nature and pioneering use of oil paint. The resulting detail, glowing colors, and subtle effects of light and texture that characterize his pictures made him one of the most famous artists of his time.

Van Eyck came from Flanders, a region that included parts of present-day Belgium, northern France, and the Netherlands. It was a prosperous area with a lively cultural life that centered around the court of the dukes of Burgundy. Van Eyck worked for many important patrons and was appointed court painter to Duke Philip the Good in 1425. He produced religious pictures and portraits, and was also entrusted with diplomatic missions. In 1430 van Eyck moved to Bruges, where he lived for the rest of his life.

Van Eyck was highly skilled at painting detail and different textures, and at capturing light effects and a realistic sense of space. These qualities first became evident in his earliest masterpiece, a large altarpiece entitled *The Adoration of the Lamb* (1432) painted with his brother Hugo. They can also be seen in his most famous work, a double portrait thought to show the marriage of the Italian merchant Giovanni Arnolfini to Giovanna Cenami (1434). Van Eyck captures the sumptuous fabrics of the

Left: The Arnolfini Marriage *(1434) by Jan van Eyck. Scholars believe that this painting was intended as a kind of legal contract for the marriage—van Eyck shows two witnesses reflected in the mirror. On the wall above he signed his name with a Latin inscription that says "Jan van Eyck was here, 1434."*

couple's clothes, the dog's coarse fur, and the bleached wood of the discarded shoes. He also captures the effect of light coming in through the window and the sense of space in the room. Many of the details also have symbolic meanings; for example, the dog is a symbol of fidelity.

The rich colors, details, and subtle light effects in van Eyck's work were enhanced by his pioneering use of oil paint. Until this time artists had mainly used tempera, a quick-drying, opaque paint made by mixing powdered pigments (colors) with egg. Oil paint was made by using oil from linseed or walnuts instead of egg. It was slow drying and could be applied in thin, transparent layers called glazes. These qualities enabled van Eyck to spend time working on details and to build up layers of glazes to create glowing colors.

SEE ALSO
♦ Bruges
♦ Flemish Painting
♦ Landscape Painting
♦ Naturalism
♦ Painting Techniques and Materials
♦ Portraiture

Families

amilies in Renaissance Europe varied according to their wealth and where they lived. A poor family in the countryside of north-western Europe usually consisted of two parents and three children, while in southern and eastern Europe a similar family often included grand-parents as well as uncles and aunts and their children. Richer families had servants. Work dominated the lives of the poor, and rich and poor alike were affected by high rates of illness and death.

On average fewer than half the children born during the Renaissance survived to the age of 15. Women usually had about six children—but many of them died while babies or while they were still young. For most people children were the only insurance policy they had against illness and old age. Children were expected to care for their parents as they grew older and less able to look after themselves.

In poor families children had to help support the family and often began working full days by age seven. In both rural and urban areas children from poor families were often sent away to work as servants, while families with a little more money might send their boys away to work as apprentices to learn a trade. Boys from noble and merchant families were given a wide-ranging education. The education of girls from these families was intended

Left: This fanciful 16th-century painting shows a bustling household in northern Europe. Richer households were often crowded places, their numbers swelled by servants and visiting relatives.

to provide religious training and the skills necessary to educate their children and run a household.

MARRIAGE

The average age of marriage for women ranged from 16 to 20 for the nobility and 18 to 22 for the working class. Men waited until they were 28 to 30. By this age it is likely that they would have had time to serve a full apprenticeship or gain a degree or professional qualification, and to have saved enough money to establish their own household, separate from that of their parents. Because illness was widespread and few effective cures were available, the death rate was high among adults as well as children, and many women died in childbirth. If a husband or wife lost their partner, it was common to remarry, often quite quickly, so that the family continued to function as a unit.

In eastern and southern Europe the situation was rather different. It was more common for children to marry young and for married sons, their wives, and families to stay in the family home. In the Balkans this practice evolved into the *zadruga*, very large family houses shared by several generations of the same family and ruled over by a patriarch (most senior man).

MEN AND WOMEN

Boys from both the wealthy and the working classes often lived away from their immediate families in order to attend school or learn a trade. For girls and women, on the other hand, life most often centered around the house and home. Apart from peasant women, who worked with their husbands in the fields, most women did not engage in separate economic activity. Although the wives of craftsmen or other men with small family businesses were

usually involved in some way—since the business was usually located in the same building as the home—on the whole they were excluded from guilds, public office, and responsibilities.

In richer families girls were not expected to contribute to household income. Instead, they were prepared to become wives and mothers. Their marriages were not based on love and romance, but were arranged to preserve or strengthen their family's economic and social standing. Young women who failed to gain a marriage proposal often entered a convent.

In rich and poor families alike, the father was head of the household. He controlled family finances, laid down the rules, administered discipline, and in return received the respect of his wife and children. Mothers were more directly involved in nurturing their children and providing their education. The ties between parents and children were reduced, however, when children were sent away to work or to receive an education.

Above: A 15th-century book illustration showing an intimate family scene. Although life was often hard and short in the Renaissance, most parents had loving relationships with their children.

SEE ALSO
♦ Children
♦ Courtiers
♦ Education

Flemish Painting

Although the Renaissance is usually associated with the artistic and cultural developments that took place in Italy during the 15th and 16th centuries, there was also a similar flowering of art in northern Europe, particularly in Flanders. Flanders—a region that includes present-day Belgium and parts of the Netherlands and France—was one of the main centers of the northern Renaissance. Flemish painters influenced Italian artists, especially in their use of oil paint.

Italian artists of the Renaissance attempted to convey ideal beauty in their paintings and sculptures. Leonardo da Vinci, Michelangelo, and other great artists were concerned with the underlying structure of things and studied perspective, proportion, and anatomy. Northern artists had a different emphasis—they worked to portray the surface appearance of the world around them. Their work grew out of the detailed, exacting tradition of medieval manuscript illumination (illustration). During the 15th century northern artists studied nature afresh and filled their pictures with details observed from everyday life.

PANEL PAINTINGS AND OIL PAINT

Flemish artists specialized in painting pictures on wooden panels—known as panel paintings—unlike Italian artists, for whom frescoes, or wall paintings, were more important. Until the 15th century most artists used a type of paint called tempera, which they made by mixing egg with powdered pigments (colors) made from ground-up plants, minerals, and bone. Tempera was fast-drying, which meant artists had to work quickly, and it was also opaque, or dull-looking.

Gradually, northern artists began to mix oil from linseed or walnuts with their pigments. The resulting oil paint

Above: The Portinari Altarpiece, painted in about 1476 by the Flemish artist Hugo van der Goes. Its landscape backgrounds and clear, detailed style are typical of Flemish painting.

could be applied in thin, transparent layers, known as glazes, which could be built up to create rich colors. Because oil paint was slow drying, it enabled artists to achieve subtle effects by blending paints and to spend time rendering the minutest detail. The Flemish painter Jan van Eyck (about 1385–1441) was the first artist to develop fully the qualities of oil paint.

PATRONS AND COMMISSIONS

One of the main reasons that art flourished in Flanders was that it was a vibrant economic center. There were many wealthy merchants, bankers, and organizations that wanted to commission art, the most powerful of whom were the dukes of Burgundy. Religious subjects were popular with patrons, but they also commissioned portraits of themselves and other family members. Up until this time artists had not painted portraits of ordinary people, and Flemish painters led the way in this new area of art, their meticulous observation and detailed style being well suited to the task.

EARLY MASTERS

Robert Campin (about 1378–1444) was among the first great Flemish artists. He is also known as the Master of Tournai, after the city in which he worked. Campin set the standard for later artists with his lifelike portraits of noblemen and women. He also gave traditional religious subjects new, everyday settings. For example, in *The Virgin and Child before a Firescreen* (about 1430) he portrayed Mary and the baby Jesus in a homely room overlooking a city. Traditionally this subject was painted with Mary sitting on a throne, often against a plain gold background. While artists usually painted holy figures with halos of

golden light around their heads, Campin used the more down-to-earth woven firescreen standing behind Mary to create the same effect.

Jan van Eyck (about 1385–1441) was the leading artist of the early northern Renaissance. He painted remarkably detailed pictures with glowing colors and subtle textures made possible by his close observation of natural appearances and his mastery of oil painting. These qualities are evident in his best-known works, such as *The Arnolfini Marriage* (1434) and *The Rolin Madonna* (1435). His skill and technical mastery made him famous throughout Europe.

Rogier van der Weyden (about 1399–1464) may have learned his trade from either Campin or van Eyck, or

Below: **The Virgin and Child before a Fire Screen,** *painted in about 1430 by Robert Campin. Campin was one of the first artists to show holy figures and Bible stories in the everyday surroundings of his own time; this became a feature of Flemish art.*

Left: **The Descent from the Cross,** *painted in about 1435 by Rogier van der Weyden. Van der Weyden painted with a clear, precise style; but here he has stripped away unnecessary detail to emphasize the power and emotion of the moment when Christ's body is taken down from the cross.*

both. His work was certainly influenced by them. Like van Eyck, van der Weyden was patronized by Philip the Good, duke of Burgundy. His skill lay in painting traditional subjects to convey fresh, powerful emotions. One of his most expressive paintings is *The Descent from the Cross* (about 1435), which shows the moment when Christ's dead body is taken down from the cross. In this large picture, painted

---

Van der Weyden's skill lay in painting traditional subjects with fresh, powerful emotions

---

as an altarpiece, van der Weyden combines clarity of line and detail with a dramatic arrangement of figures who emphasize Christ's suffering through their grief-stricken poses. Christ's mother Mary faints, and her pose

mirrors the broken body of Christ above her; Mary Magdalen, on the right, contorts her body in an extraordinary display of grief. Van der Weyden based the appearance of his painting on carved wooden altarpieces that were popular in northern Europe.

Van der Weyden had a flourishing workshop where many young artists learned their trade. He probably trained several other major Flemish painters, including Dieric Bouts (about 1415–1475) and the German-born Hans Memling (about 1430–1494), who worked in Bruges.

Hugo van der Goes (about 1436–1482) was a major figure in northern art in the late 15th century. He is best known for several large-scale works, including the *Portinari Altarpiece* (shown on page 7), painted in about 1476 for the Italian banker Tommaso Portinari. The altarpiece is a triptych, which means it consists of three panels: a central panel and two smaller side panels, or wings, that can be closed.

The backs of the wings, seen when they are closed, are painted with the Annunciation, the moment when the angel Gabriel announces to Mary that she will give birth to Jesus. The figures of Gabriel and Mary are painted to look like sculptures, in imitation of carved altarpieces. When the wings are open, they reveal a scene painted in brilliant oil colors showing the Nativity, when the three shepherds and three kings came to see the newly born baby Jesus in the stable. The insides of the two wings show Tommaso and his family with their patron saints.

In the early Renaissance Flemish and Italian painting developed relatively independently. In the 16th century, however, there was more interchange between the two. Quentin Massys (about 1465–1530) was a Flemish artist who drew inspiration from both traditions. His satirical portraits of wealthy merchants and bankers are his most famous works.

NEW DIRECTIONS

Around the end of the 15th century Hieronymus Bosch (about 1450–1516) broke the mold of Flemish art. He came from 's-Hertogenbosch (from which he took his name), a town near Antwerp. Although 's-Hertogenbosch was not a leading cultural center, Bosch attracted many important patrons. His paintings were unlike anything that had gone before. They show nightmare scenes in which tiny human figures are tempted or tortured by demons and fantastic creatures. Bosch painted each detail of his disturbing fantasies with a lifelike accuracy and precision, as if he was working from everyday life.

Many artists were influenced by Bosch's fantastic imagery, including Pieter Bruegel the Elder (about 1525–1569). Bruegel painted pictures that

dealt with the folly of man, as Bosch had done, but he is best known for his depictions of peasant life in the countryside of northern Europe. He even painted Bible stories as if they were taking place in 16th-century Flemish villages. In pictures such as *Hunters in the Snow* (1565) Bruegel devoted much of the painting to showing the countryside. Although Flemish artists had painted landscape as the background to religious pictures from the 15th century, few had given it such prominence.

Bruegel's work marked the end of a brilliant period in Flemish art. The technical advances made by artists in the use of oil paint spread throughout Europe, as did their sensitive depiction of the detail of everyday life, landscape, and portraiture.

Above: Bosch's painting **The Temptation of Saint Anthony** *shows a nightmarish scene of hellfire, goblins, and demons who attack the saint.*

SEE ALSO
♦ Bosch
♦ Bruegel, Pieter the Elder
♦ Eyck, Jan van
♦ Landscape Painting
♦ Painting Techniques and Materials
♦ Portraiture

Florence

Situated on the Arno River in Tuscany, Florence was one of the great cities of the Renaissance. It was prosperous and powerful, especially under the rule of the Medici family in the 15th century. It was renowned for its beautiful buildings, such as the Pitti and Uffizi palaces, the Santa Croce church, and the Duomo, or cathedral, with its magnificent dome. Florence was also the home of a number of brilliant intellectuals, painters, and sculptors, including the poet Dante, the artist Leonardo da Vinci, and the political thinker Niccolò Machiavelli.

Florence was founded in 59 B.C. by the Roman general Julius Caesar. Its name means "flourishing," and that is exactly what the city did from the 12th century onward. From its position on the Arno River, which connected it with Pisa and the coast, Florence grew prosperous on trade. Its specialty was textiles. Florentine merchants would go abroad and bring back wool and cloth from countries such as England and Flanders. The raw materials were then processed and dyed with brilliant colors and exported. The other main foundation of the city's wealth was banking. Great banking families, such as the Medici, Peruzzi, and Bardi, built up a network of contacts all over Europe and became renowned as international financiers. From 1252 the city's gold coin, the florin, was in use throughout the continent.

PLAGUE AND FAMINE

By the first half of the 14th century Florence had become one of the largest cities of Europe, with a population of about 100,000 citizens. Then in 1348 disaster struck. The plague known as the Black Death, which was to devastate Europe, descended on Florence and

Above: The city of Florence as it appears today. The dome of the city's cathedral, built by the architect Filippo Brunelleschi in the 15th century, still dominates Florence's skyline on the right of the picture, while the famous Ponte Vecchio, or Old Bridge, over the Arno River can be seen on the left.

Right: A 17th-century fresco (wall painting) showing Lorenzo de Medici, ruler of Florence, surrounded by some of the many artists whose work he commissioned. On the right of the picture Michelangelo presents one of his sculptures to Lorenzo.

killed half the population. In the aftermath the city suffered a long downward turn in its finances as well as considerable social unrest. Periods of famine prompted riots among the poor, who had no form of political representation. The situation was made worse by further bouts of the plague.

Toward the end of the century Florence also faced danger from the powerful city of Milan to the north. Milan at this time was governed by Giangaleazzo Visconti, who controlled much of northern Italy. He was determined to get his hands on Florence. By 1402 he was ready to

THE GUILDS OF FLORENCE

During much of the Renaissance Florence was a republic—that is, it was governed not by a king or prince but by a group of citizens. Its rulers tended to come from a small number of powerful families and guilds, which were organized groups of merchants, businessmen, or craftsmen.

There were seven major guilds in Florence, including those of the wool merchants, the weavers, and the bankers, and twice as many minor guilds. The minor guilds were those of groups such as bakers, cobblers, and carpenters. Each guild elected its own officials and had its own flag and even a church to

worship in. Apart from these skilled workers there were the manual laborers—who made up most of the population—who did relatively unskilled jobs such as unloading and hauling bales of wool or spinning or dyeing cloth.

A constant friction existed between the major guilds, which were very wealthy, and the minor guilds, which were less wealthy but greater in number. In 1378 low-paid wool workers known as the Ciompi staged a revolt and overthrew the government. However, they were defeated in the same year, and the major guilds soon regained their grip on power.

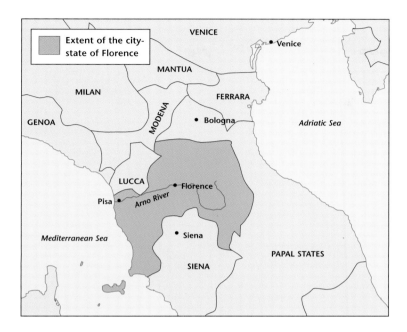

attack the city. Before Visconti could strike, however, he died of a fever, and Florence was saved.

COSIMO DE MEDICI

For the relieved Florentines this escape marked a new era of prosperity until the 1420s, when another war with Milan and financial difficulties created political problems within the city. Florence's fortunes recovered after Cosimo de Medici (1389–1464), a member of a powerful Florentine family, assumed power in 1434. The city now entered a 50-year period when it became the leading cultural and intellectual center in Italy.

Cosimo himself, who was fabulously rich through his banking and other interests, never actually made himself ruler of the city. Instead, he controlled it through his numerous supporters, who held key political positions. Cosimo was a great patron of the arts and had new churches and palaces built and older ones renovated. He supported artists such as the sculptor Donatello and the painter Fra Angelico. He was also a clever

Above: This map shows the extent of the city-state of Florence in the late 15th century.

Below: A joust taking place in Florence's Piazza Santa Croce in the 16th century. The city arranged many entertainments for its citizens.

statesman. After his death in 1464 the Florentines hailed him as *pater patriae*—"father of his country."

Cosimo's son Piero took over from his father for only five years before he died in 1469. He was succeeded by his own son Lorenzo (1449–1492), a poet as well as a shrewd politician, who was later known as "the Magnificent." By this time the people of Florence could admire numerous beautiful civic and religious buildings and enjoy frequent parades and carnivals, when people took part in processions along the streets wearing costumes and masks and carrying colorful banners.

FLORENCE PROSPERS

Lorenzo's reign coincided with a prosperous period of Florence's history. An Italian writer of the period noted that the city included 33 banks, 44 shops run by goldsmiths and jewelers, 84 by cabinetmakers, and 270 by wool merchants. The wealthy lived in palatial houses in town or retreated to grand villas in the countryside to read or go hawking and hunting.

Lorenzo continued to rule until his death in 1492. He was lucky, however, to escape being assassinated during his reign. The Pazzi family and their

followers resented the Medici's grip on power and wanted to govern the city themselves. So they attacked Lorenzo and his brother Giuliano while they were at church. Giuliano was killed, but Lorenzo escaped. The attackers were then hunted down by the Florentine people and put to death.

FLORENCE IN DECLINE

By the time Lorenzo died the golden age of Florence had faded. Florentine merchants found that the English and the Flemish were less reliant on their textiles. Trade with the East also declined. Then in 1494 the city experienced fresh upheavals when the French king Charles VIII, backed by the Medici's enemies, forced the family into exile. In their absence leadership of the city fell to a fiery Dominican monk named Savonarola (1452–1498), who preached that all luxuries and expensive clothes and practices such as gambling were immoral. He organized

---

In the absence of the Medici leadership of the city fell to a fiery Dominican monk named Savonarola

---

the "bonfire of vanities," that is, the burning of playing cards, musical instruments, and other objects he felt distracted people from living in a holy way. Eventually, the Florentines grew angry with Savonarola. With the backing of Pope Alexander VI, whom Savonarola had also verbally attacked, they hanged and burned him.

The Medici returned to the city in 1512 and again took control of Florentine politics. Their influence

during this period also extended to the church when one of Lorenzo's sons, and then one of his nephews, became pope. By this time the great days of Renaissance Florence were nearly over. But it had one last flourish during the reign of another Cosimo de Medici (1519–1574), known as "the Great," who took the title of duke of Florence in 1537. Cosimo conquered new lands for Florence, gaining control of much of Tuscany. He also commissioned works by many distinguished artists, including Michelangelo and Bronzino, built and refurbished palaces, and created the famous Boboli Gardens, with their spectacular statues, grottoes, and fountains

In 1564, with a decade of his life still remaining, Cosimo allowed his son Francesco to take over the day-to-day running of the city. By the time he died in 1574, Florence's vitality, so evident in the 15th century, had largely evaporated. However, the city's major contribution to the culture of Europe can still be seen in its magnificent art and architecture.

Above: This 16th-century painting shows the Dominican monk Savonarola being burned for heresy. Savonarola was the virtual ruler of Florence for several years, but his attacks on the pope led to his downfall.

SEE ALSO

Food and Drink

In the Renaissance period the rich benefited from an ever-increasing range of foods as European explorers brought back spices, fruits, vegetables, and meats from the East Indies and, in the 16th century, from the recently discovered Americas. The new foods included tomatoes, peppers, potatoes, corn (maize), ginger, nutmeg, and turkeys. Yet while the wealthy enjoyed extravagant foods, the diet of the ordinary people remained monotonous and scarcely adequate, especially in the winter.

The diet of peasants was dominated by grain—wheat, oats, barley, and millet —that was made into coarse bread. A typical peasant meal consisted of thin vegetable soup made from peas, beans, or cabbage, eaten with bread. This basic diet was sometimes supplemented by eggs and cheese. Meat— normally pork—was a rare delicacy. Water and milk were not safe to drink; everyone, including small children, drank alcohol in the form of ale (a kind of weak beer), cider (fermented apple juice), or mead (a drink made from honey and water).

Food storage was often a problem. Rats and mice attacked grain, weevils burrowed into beans, bacon turned rancid, and cheese turned moldy. During the winter peasants relied on food that they had preserved earlier in the year. Meat was salted or cured over open fires. Vegetables and pulses, such as peas and beans, were dried, bottled, and preserved in vinegar. Fresh fruit and vegetables, often plentiful enough

in the summer months, were simply not available in the winter, and everyone's health suffered.

THE FEASTS OF THE RICH

A table groaning with a vast amount of exotic, elaborately prepared food was an obvious way to display wealth, and the lavish feasts of medieval times continued to be an important part of Renaissance life. Wealthy townspeople ate an astonishing amount, and variety, on special occasions. In the early 16th century 50 guests at a feast held by a London guild consumed 36 chickens, one swan, four geese, and two rumps of beef—and that was just the meat!

Banquets held on important state occasions were even more elaborate. At the coronation of England's Henry IV in 1399 guests were presented with a bewildering choice of boar's head (complete with gilded tusks), heron,

Above: This 15th-century fresco (wall painting) shows an Italian vegetable market. In Renaissance times vegetables, along with bread, were the staple food of the poor—meat was a rare luxury.

sturgeon, venison, stuffed suckling pig, peacocks (roasted whole and served in full plumage), grilled pork pastries, quinces in syrup, and custard pies.

Meat was served with spicy dipping sauces, often to disguise the fact that it had been salted or was not quite fresh. The sauces were made from exotic spices such as ginger, saffron, cloves, cardamom, and cinnamon. Special sauce-makers were important members of the kitchen staff in wealthy households. Food was washed down with wine, which came predominantly from France.

DIET AND HEALTH

People were just beginning to understand that overeating on this scale was bad for their health. By the 16th century some governments tried to limit the number of dishes served at weddings or special occasions. In 16th-century Italy eating habits started to become more restrained. Variety was supplied by an impressive array of basic ingredients rather than an overwhelming range of spices.

RECIPE BOOKS

The invention of printing brought an array of popular books dedicated to health and diet, housekeeping, and cooking. Recipes were written in the languages of ordinary people rather than Latin. Through these books it is possible to trace the gradual change from medieval to modern cookery. The recipes in *A Booke of Cookry Very Necessary for All Such as Delight Therein Gathered by A.W.* (1584) still reveal a medieval delight in spices, sugar, and elaborate fruit and meat combinations. However, some 30 years later *The English Hus-wife* (1615) by Gervase Markham appeared. Aimed at women who had to cater for large country houses, it recommended that they should prepare plain but satisfying food using home-grown ingredients.

Table manners started to improve as the boisterous feasts of the medieval world were replaced by more civilized meals. Trenchers—thick slices of bread that served as plates—were replaced with real plates of silver, pewter, and pottery. Tables were laid with linen tablecloths and napkins. People stopped eating with their fingers, and two-pronged forks were introduced.

Left: This painting by the 16th-century Flemish artist Jan Bruegel shows the kind of dishes the wealthy enjoyed—including a peacock pie, complete with tail feathers.

SEE ALSO

♦ Agriculture
♦ Americas
♦ Daily Life
♦ Exploration
♦ Trade

Fortifications

During the Renaissance period the type of fortifications used changed dramatically in response to the development of gunpowder and cannon. The tall stone battlements and towers built to protect castles and towns in the late Middle Ages were no longer enough to withstand enemy attack. From the 15th century military engineers constructed massive earth defenses and sank their fortresses into the ground to prevent their walls from being battered by cannon fire.

In the late Middle Ages castles were built with huge stone walls to protect them. They often had a strong, square keep at the center, where the lord, his family, and followers lived, surrounded by one or more rings of protective walls or ramparts. These walls were thick and tall, with narrow slit openings, overhanging galleries, and battlements on top for archers to shoot from. They were further protected by tall towers and deep moats. Moats kept attackers away from the walls, making it more difficult for them to scale the ramparts using wooden siege towers or to tunnel under them. Some medieval fortresses, such as the Crusader castle Krak de Chevaliers in Lebanon, were virtually impenetrable and withstood sieges months and even years long.

Below: The Mastio della Rocca, an Italian fortress designed by the military architect Antonio da Sangallo the Elder. Its low, thick walls are typical of the Renaissance period, when fortresses had to withstand heavy cannon fire.

All this changed in the 15th century, when cannons were developed that were capable of firing stone and metal cannon balls large distances with great force using gunpowder. The first cannons, developed toward the end of the 14th century, were unwieldy and were mainly used for defense rather than in the field for attack. Castles were modified to accommodate gun ports with reinforced platforms to withstand the weight and recoil (backward movement) of the cannon when it was fired. By the start of the 15th century, however, technological developments resulted in an effective bronze cannon that could be used for attacking.

These siege cannons could be positioned much further from the castle wall than the huge catapults that had been used in medieval warfare—and thus much further from defensive fire—and were also capable of battering down the stone walls in a much shorter time. The German Frederick I of Brandenburg was one of the first rulers to use cannons systematically to defeat his enemies. The French king Charles VII deployed them against the English in the Hundred Years' War, while his grandson Charles VIII used them when he invaded Italy in 1494. Using cannons, his troops took the key Italian fortress of Monte San Giovanni in just eight hours—it had previously withstood a siege for seven years.

PROTECTION AGAINST CANNONS

Military engineers needed to come up with a solution. At first they fitted more defensive cannons into their castles and reduced the height of their walls to make them less vulnerable to battering. Soon, however, the Italians entirely rethought the design of their fortifications. They sank the fortress

into the ground behind a deep ditch and built huge sloping earth ramparts around it. The soft earth absorbed cannon shot much better than hard stone walls, which tended to shatter, and the slope further deflected cannon fire and could be defended by placing gun ports along the top.

The defensive area around the fortress was also enlarged with outworks of ditches and earth ramparts in order to keep the enemy cannons as far away as possible and so reduce the impact of their fire. These ditches were protected with gun ports set in low projections that were polygonal, or many-sided, in shape to afford comprehensive cover and inflict maximum damage on advancing troops.

The scale and complexity of these earthen outworks increased steadily through the course of the 16th century as attacking armies became larger and more heavily armed. However, the basic type of fortress developed in the Renaissance, with its sunken profile and elaborate pattern of earthen outworks, was used until the 19th century, when new developments in artillery made it obsolete.

Above: This engraving shows the city of Vienna in the late 16th century. It is surrounded by both a moat and angled, low walls. These fortifications helped the city withstand a siege by the Ottoman Turks in 1529.

SEE ALSO
♦ Arms and Armor
♦ Warfare

France

At the beginning of the 15th century France was not a well-defined state. Some areas that are part of present-day France were self-ruling duchies or disputed territories. The independent duchy of Britanny, in the west, did not come under the rule of the French crown until 1491. In the east there was a blurred border with the powerful duchy of Burgundy. To the northeast peasants could take advantage of the uncertain border with the Holy Roman Empire to avoid paying taxes to either ruler. France did not even have a common language—the *langue d'oïl* was spoken in the north and the *langue d'oc* in the south.

Struggles for control of economically important areas, such as the county of Flanders in the northwest, dominated the first half of the 15th century. The main preoccupation of the French kings at this time was to keep French territory out of English hands. The Hundred Years' War between France and England had begun in 1337. Periods of peace had alternated with periods of war as a succession of English monarchs made bids to claim the French crown, and several areas of land changed hands many times.

In 1415 the young English king Henry V (ruled 1413–1422) revived England's efforts. With Henry's daring victory over the French at the battle of

Below: This 15th-century manuscript illustration shows English and French troops fighting at the battle of Agincourt in 1415. The English, under Henry V, won a great victory that temporarily swung the tide of the Hundred Years' War in their favor.

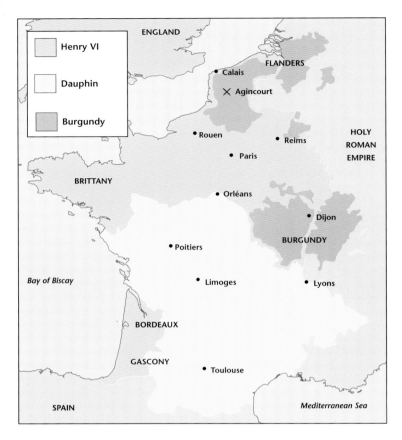

Above: This map shows the areas of France loyal to Henry VI of England, the dauphin (Charles, heir to the French throne), and the duke of Burgundy in 1429, the year of the siege of Orléans.

break up the English siege of Orléans in 1429. Charles VII was crowned king the same year, and the tide of the war turned in France's favor. Joan of Arc, however, was captured by the Burgundians, sold to the English, and burned at the stake for heresy in 1431. She became a powerful symbol of a growing sense of French nationhood.

In 1453 the Hundred Years' War came to an end with the surrender of

---

Joan of Arc became a powerful symbol of a growing sense of French nationhood

---

Gascony and Bordeaux to the French. Only the port of Calais remained in English hands. France emerged stronger and more united in the second half of the 15th century, a period of relative calm. Between the end of the Hundred Years' War and the beginning of the Wars of Religion in 1562 little fighting took place on French soil. The countryside began to recover—not only from the ravages of war, but also from plague. The population of France had been cut in half between 1330 and 1450 by the Black Death, but between 1450 and 1560 it revived and doubled. There were still occasional outbreaks of plague, but they were limited.

CROWN AND NOBILITY

Throughout western Europe the period from 1460 to 1600 saw a general decline in the power of the nobility and the emergence of monarchs who had a firmer control of their country. Despite this trend, France still saw a fierce struggle between the crown and the nobility in the second half of the 15th

Agincourt the future of the French crown became uncertain. In the following years the towns of Falaise, Cherbourg, Rouen, and Pontoise surrendered to the English. In May 1420 the French king Charles VI (ruled 1380–1422) was forced to agree to the Treaty of Troyes, by which Henry became heir to the French throne. Henry died before he could wear the French crown. Instead, when Charles VI died in 1422, the throne passed to Henry V's baby son, King Henry VI of England. However Charles VI's son, also called Charles, proclaimed himself king as well.

JOAN OF ARC

It took a young peasant girl, Joan of Arc (about 1412–1431), to rally the French and put Charles on the throne. Led by visions of saints who told her to come to Charles' aid, she led French troops to

century. Louis XI (ruled 1461–1483) made considerable attempts to curb the power of the nobles. In response the dukes of Alençon, Burgundy, Bourbon, and Lorraine joined forces and tried to topple their king. He defeated them in battle at Nancy in 1477.

When Charles the Bold became duke of Burgundy in 1467, Louis XI had another powerful and dangerous noble to contend with. Charles aimed to establish a separate Burgundian kingdom, and in 1474 fighting broke out between Burgundy and France. A year later Charles supported an English invasion. The alliance between England and Burgundy posed a serious threat to the unity of France. To counter the threat, Louis XI was forced to pay an annual fee to Edward IV of England to persuade him to stay at home. Charles VIII continued the tradition of paying the English king to abandon his claim to the French crown.

FRANCIS I AND HENRY II

When Francis I (ruled 1515–1547) took the throne, an era of strong, effective personal monarchy began. Both Francis and his successor Henry II (ruled 1547–1559) enjoyed long reigns.

Above: The dukes of Alençon, Burgundy, and Bourbon, together with other nobles, swear an oath of alliance against King Louis XI in 1465.

Francis I's flamboyant personality boosted France's international standing in the 16th century. He was renowned for his patronage of the arts, the grandeur of his palace at Fontaine-bleau, and his stream of mistresses. When Henry II succeeded Francis, the tone of the court changed. He put a stop to many of the entertainments and

THE HOUSE OF BOURBON

The house of Bourbon was the most powerful noble family in France in the early 16th century. In 1521 the Bourbon lands comprised three duchies, seven counties, two vicomtés, and seven lordships, forming a block of territories in central France. Within his territory the duke was all-powerful—he could raise troops, levy taxes, and dispense justice.

Charles, eighth duke of Bourbon (1490–1527), was appointed constable of France when Francis I became king, but by 1521 relations between them had soured. When Francis tried to claim Bourbon

territory for the crown, Charles turned traitor and plotted with the Holy Roman emperor and Henry VIII of England against Francis. When news of the alliance became known, the duke fled to Spain, where he became a general in the emperor's army. In 1524 the duke fought in the battle of Pavia, in which the French forces were defeated and Francis I taken prisoner.

The Bourbon family remained a power in French politics, and in 1589 the Bourbon Henry of Navarre became king of France. The family continued to rule the country until 1792 and again from 1814 to 1848.

pledged to devote his time to "grave and virtuous thoughts."

Both Francis and Henry waged a number of wars with the Spanish king and Holy Roman emperor Charles V over Italian territory. The Italian Wars placed a serious financial drain on the French, who gained very little from them. In the Treaty of Cateau-Cambresis, signed by Henry II in 1559, France gave up all its conquests except Toul, Metz, and Verdun. This left Spain in control of most of Italy.

THE ROLE OF A KING

The reigns of the strong-willed and capable Francis and Henry helped reestablish the authority of the French monarchy. Two books that attempted to define the exact role of the king were written for Francis I at the start of his reign—Claude de Seyssel's *La Monarchie de France* ("The Monarchy of France") and Guillaume Budé's *L'Institution du Prince* ("The Role of a Prince"). Seyssel admired the French monarchy because its actions could be at least partially controlled by the nobles. They sat in the Parlement of Paris, which was important because the king needed its approval to raise new taxes. Budé favored an all-powerful monarchy. He believed that the only influence on the actions of a king should be the thought of how his deeds would be judged by later generations.

The French government still resembled Seyssel's model, but a strong monarch like Francis could and did try to override the Parlement. The king's

THE WORKS OF RABELAIS

François Rabelais (1494–1553) was a Franciscan monk whose humanist studies brought him into conflict with the church. In 1524 he asked Pope Clement VII to let him transfer to the Benedictine order, because the Franciscans frowned on his wide-ranging studies in science, medicine, astronomy, and botany.

In 1532 Rabelais published *Pantagruel*, a comic tale about a giant. The book became hugely popular and was greatly enjoyed by King Francis I. In 1534 Rabelais followed it with *Gargantua*, which charted the adventures of Pantagruel's father. Both tales parodied the tales about heroic knights that had been popular in medieval times and mixed lively humor with comment about contemporary political and religious issues. Rabelais's mockery of the Catholic church led the church authorities to condemn the books. Rabelais's later works, *Tiers Livre* ("Third Book") and *Quart Livre* ("Fourth Book"), were published in the 1540s. In order to escape the attention of the French church authorities, he made many trips to Italy, where he picked up new ideas. He is remembered as a great storyteller and satirist whose work is a shining example of the questioning spirit of the Renaissance.

Above: This illustration from an 18th-century edition of Rabelais's Gargantua *shows the giant of the title at dinner. A sharp satire, the book contains humorous attacks on lazy clerics, greedy lawyers, and ignorant doctors.*

council, or *conseil d'etat*, was comprised of nobles, although admission to the council was by royal invitation only. There was also an inner ring consisting of the king's close friends and advisers, whom he could consult secretly.

RELIGIOUS DIVISIONS

The confidence of the French monarchy dipped in the second half of the 16th century. After the death of Henry II France was ruled by the short-lived 15-year-old Francis II (ruled 1559–1560). He was succeeded by his 10-year-old brother Charles IX (ruled 1560–1574). At first Charles' mother Catherine de Medici ruled France as regent. Even when Charles came of age in 1563, Catherine continued to wield an enormous amount of power, far more than the king himself.

The tensions between the crown and nobility came to a head with the outbreak of civil war in 1562. Many French nobles followed Martin Luther and John Calvin's lead to leave the Catholic church and take up the Protestant faith. Others, such as the influential Guise family, became champions of Catholicism. The old struggles for power between various noble factions were bloodily revived— this time along religious lines.

The Wars of Religion between the Huguenots (Protestants) and Catholics lasted from 1562 until 1598. The worst incident was the Saint Bartholomew's Day Massacre on August 24, 1572, when hundreds of Huguenots were killed by a Catholic mob in Paris. The killings spread through the country, and nearly 20,000 people died. The fiercely Catholic Catherine de Medici was blamed for inflaming the situation. It was not until 1570 and the Peace of Saint Germain-en-Laye that the Huguenots gained conditional freedom of worship in France.

In 1574 Henry III, another son of Catherine de Medici, became king of France. In 1585 he banned the Protestant religion, plunging the country into further civil strife. An end to the hostilities came when Henry of Navarre (ruled 1589–1610), who had been raised a Protestant, became King Henry IV of France in 1589. In 1593 Henry converted to Catholicism, allegedly saying, "Paris is worth a mass." In 1598 he issued the Edict of Nantes, which gave Huguenots the same political rights as Catholics.

Above: This 16th-century painting shows members of the Holy League marching through Paris. The league, composed of Catholics, was organized in 1576 by the duke of Guise to fight the Huguenots, or Protestants.

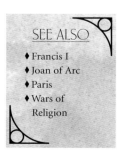

SEE ALSO
- Francis I
- Joan of Arc
- Paris
- Wars of Religion

Francis I

Above: This portrait of Francis I is by Jean Clouet, who was the official painter to the king. He was just one of many artists patronized by Francis during his reign.

Francis I of France (1494–1547) was born Francis of Angoulême and inherited the French crown at the age of 20. He ruled France for the next 32 years, during which time he was almost constantly at war, mostly with his great rival the Holy Roman emperor Charles V. Francis was also a generous patron of the arts and learning, and established a brilliant court where painters, musicians, poets, and scholars mingled with cultured lords and ladies.

Francis was born in the town of Cognac, the son of Charles of Angoulême and Louise of Savoy. His father died when Francis was just two years old, and he and his sister Marguerite (who was later to be queen of Navarre) were brought up by their mother. At the age of four Francis became heir to the French throne when his cousin was crowned Louis XII.

The young Francis showed a great interest in the courtly life and ways of a knight, listening to tales and songs of chivalry. When he was 18, Louis sent him to help the French army defend its borders from attack. This suited Francis, who welcomed the opportunity to learn about warfare.

A YOUNG BRIDE

A year later Francis married Louis's 14-year-old daughter Claude. This move annoyed Charles of Austria—the future Holy Roman emperor Charles V—who had been promised Claude's hand in marriage by her mother, Anne of Brittany. Shortly after the wedding Louis XII died, and on January 1, 1515, Francis became king of France. He was crowned in the Notre-Dame Cathedral at Reims and celebrated his kingship with a ceremonial procession into Paris and a series of feasts. But just six months later Francis was once again on the battlefield.

He led an army across the Alps and rode at the head of his cavalry when they captured the duchy of Milan. He then asked to be knighted by the captain who had masterminded this great victory, the famous Chevalier de Bayard, the "knight without fear."

While he was in Italy, Francis was received by Pope Leo X and was impressed by the brilliant papal court. Inspired by this gathering of scholars and artists, and by the succession of banquets and entertainments held by the pope, Francis decided to have a glittering court of his own. He arranged for Leonardo da Vinci and other Italian artists to come to his court

---

Francis arranged for Leonardo da Vinci to come to his court in France

---

in France and bring some of their paintings with them. Francis granted a yearly allowance to Leonardo and began to build up a collection of works by artists like Michelangelo and Titian.

THE CHÂTEAU DE BLOIS

Thanks to his wealth Francis was able to commission many works by Italian Renaissance artists and architects. One example can be seen at the Château de Blois in the Loire Valley. There he had a great eight-sided staircase built. Topped by a gallery overlooking the castle's courtyard, the staircase is a masterpiece of French Renaissance architecture. At nearby Château de Chambord Francis knocked down an old hunting lodge and turned it into a magnificent palace with a central keep, roof terraces, towers, and 365 chimneys. Some of its features, including a grand double staircase, may have originally been designed by Leonardo da Vinci. At Blois and Chambord Francis's personal emblem of a salamander was incorporated into many of the decorations.

In 1519 the Holy Roman emperor Maximilian died. Francis hoped to become his successor, but the 19-year-old Charles of Austria, who by now was also king of Spain, was elected emperor instead. The two young men were to be bitter rivals for the next 27 years, resulting in many years of brutal warfare, separated by a few periods of uneasy peace. At the battle of Pavia in 1525 the emperor's forces defeated the French, and Francis was wounded and taken prisoner. He wrote to his mother: "All I have left is my honor and my life." He was released from prison a year later, after reluctantly agreeing to give up French lands to the Holy Roman

Below: The eight-sided staircase built by Francis I at the Château de Blois in the Loire valley. It is considered one of the great examples of French Renaissance architecture.

THE SCHOOL OF FONTAINEBLEAU

Francis hired talented Italian painters to decorate his beautiful palace at Fontainebleau. The work began in 1528 and continued until after the king's death in 1547. Much of it was done by Giovanni Battista Rosso (1495–1540) and Francesco Primaticcio (about 1504–1570), who adapted their styles to suit the king's taste. Rosso developed a special technique of wall decoration, molding stucco (fine plaster) into shapes that looked like leather straps or rolled parchment. Primaticcio specialized in painting elongated human figures, and he traveled to Rome to buy sculptures or have casts of them made for Francis. Rosso and Primaticcio were helped by Niccolò dell' Abbate (about 1512–1571), as well as French and Flemish artists. Their work formed a distinctive branch of the style called mannerism, and together they are known as the School of Fontainebleau.

Left: The Francis I Gallery at the Château de Fontainebleau, decorated with frescoes (wall paintings) and plaster sculptures.

Empire. He also had to hand over his two young sons as hostages; they were held prisoner for four years.

Despite these setbacks Francis continued to patronize the arts and lead the life of a royal knight. He went on hunting trips all over France, entertained artists and scholars at his court, and gave commissions to architects and builders. One of his favorite hunting lodges outside Paris was turned into the Château de Fontainebleau. It was modeled on Florentine and Roman architecture, and became the official residence for French royalty for centuries. In 1530 Francis founded the Collège de France in Paris, which specialized in the teaching of Greek, Hebrew, and mathematics.

Even though he himself was a Catholic, Francis was tolerant of Protestants for much of his reign. He admired the Dutch humanist Erasmus, and he had also read works by the German Protestant reformer Philipp Melanchthon. However, while his sister Marguerite of Navarre supported the Protestant Reformation, his ministers and advisers were all fervent Catholics. In 1534 Francis was deeply offended by the actions of some extreme Protestants who did not support the monarchy and were thought to be republicans (people who wanted to do away with the monarchy). Before long the reformers were being persecuted, and many were convicted of heresy and burned at the stake.

By this time the king himself was sick and weak. In his final year he was carried from one palace to another on a litter before dying at Rambouillet in 1547. He was succeeded by his son, who was crowned Henry II.

SEE ALSO

♦ Charles V
♦ France
♦ French Art
♦ Hapsburg Dynasty
♦ Holy Roman Empire
♦ Humanism
♦ Leonardo da Vinci
♦ Mannerism
♦ Marguerite of Navarre
♦ Reformation

Free Cities

By the end of the 15th century there were about 3,000 towns and cities in the Holy Roman Empire, of which about 100 possessed the title of "free city." Among the most important were Lübeck, Strasbourg, Cologne, and Basel. Free cities were distinguished by the fact that they possessed charters permitting them to govern themselves. These charters were granted by the Holy Roman emperor himself. They freed the cities from the authority of dukes, counts, archbishops, and all other rulers apart from the emperor. Because the empire was relatively weak at the time, the free cities were practically independent states.

Free cities were governed by councils presided over by a burgermeister, or mayor. These institutions were not very democratic. No free city permitted all of its residents to participate in government. The right to sit on the town council was restricted to an elite few. Some councils were dominated by rich merchants and bankers, who were members of associations known as merchant guilds. In other towns merchants shared power with guilds of craftsmen, who, depending on the nature of the local economy, could also be quite wealthy. The nobility also played an important role in the running of a city—often certain families would dominate a particular town's council for generations.

Free cities generally enjoyed a great deal of financial independence. For example, they often minted their own coins. That could be a very profitable enterprise. Coins issued in the name of a town were considered to be evidence

Below: The city of Lübeck in northern Germany. In the 14th and 15th centuries Lübeck was the headquarters of the Hanseatic League, an important association of trading towns.

COLOGNE

Cologne was one of the most important free cities of the Renaissance. It was founded in Roman times and by the 13th century had grown extremely prosperous through trade. At this time the city was controlled by its archbishop, whose position was strengthened by the fact that he was one of the electors entitled to choose the Holy Roman emperor. However, there was considerable tension between the archbishop and the wealthy merchants who controlled the city's trade, and in 1288 supporters of the two factions clashed at the battle of Worringen. The merchants were victorious, and after this point Cologne governed itself, although it was only officially recognized as a free city by the emperor in 1475.

To begin with the government of the city lay in the hands of the nobility, but in 1396 a new constitution was declared in which the 22 most important guilds elected a town council. Cologne flourished, thanks mainly to the fact that it was situated on both the Rhine River and a major overland trade route. The city was an important member of the Hanseatic League and had thriving textile and metalworking industries. It continued to be economically successful throughout the 16th century.

of its importance. City officials supervised the collection of regular taxes and had the authority to levy special ones for well-defined purposes such as repairing walls and maintaining public buildings. The free cities were also obliged to gather and pay certain taxes directly to the emperor. There was a special tax to help pay for the emperor's coronation, while another source of revenue was the tolls that people paid to travel on imperial roads and bridges.

THE HANSEATIC LEAGUE

During the Renaissance German cities often formed confederations. The most famous of them was the Hanseatic League, a network of trading towns that stretched all across northern Europe. The confederation came into being in the 13th century, when German merchants formed alliances so that they could afford to protect themselves against robbers and pirates. The Hanseatic League grew to be extremely rich and powerful. One of its most important members was the free city of Lübeck, located near the Baltic coast. The citizens of Lübeck created

Below: This map shows some of the most important free cities in the Holy Roman Empire during the period of the Renaissance.

their own set of laws and system of government, which were used as a model by many other cities in the area.

Town councils were also responsible for the military organization of their cities. The Hanseatic League did not hesitate to go to war against nearby Scandinavian kingdoms when it saw a threat to its commercial interests. In

1419 the league even entered into hostilities against the distant kingdom of Castile in Spain. Cities had urban militias, whose original purpose was to defend the town. During the 15th century, however, many of them became increasingly aggressive, conquering the surrounding countryside and carving out city-states. Some of the confederations that were formed during the Renaissance turned into formidable military alliances.

THE SWISS CONFEDERATION

The most important of these alliances was the Swiss Confederation, a league of independent farming communities that was joined by the free cities of Zurich, Bern, and later, Basel. Although there were occasional disputes within the alliance, the various cities and regions generally united to repel foreign attacks. The powerful city of Bern lay on the western side of the confederation, while Zurich lay to the northeast, and together they protected the confederation against attacks from aggressive neighbors like Austria and Burgundy. The Swiss quickly earned a reputation as ferocious fighters and were widely used as mercenaries in the 15th and 16th centuries.

Free cities played an extremely important role in the spread of the Reformation. The works of Luther were printed in large numbers in cities such as Strasbourg and Basel. By the 1530s over half of the free cities had become Protestant, even though they were supposed to be under the control of the emperor Charles V, who was strongly committed to Catholicism. In 1555 the Peace of Augsburg established the principle that a city council could determine which of the two religions its inhabitants practiced.

Above: The Fuggerie, Europe's oldest housing project for the poor, in the former free city of Augsburg. It was paid for by the wealthy Fugger banking family.

SEE ALSO

♦ Bavaria
♦ Germany
♦ Government, Systems of
♦ Holy Roman Empire
♦ Protestantism
♦ Reformation
♦ Towns
♦ Trade

French Art

During the 15th century French artists worked in the elaborate Gothic style that had flourished in the late Middle Ages. They were famed for their richly colored book illustrations and stained glass. However, by the end of the 15th century France was no longer a leading center for art, and Italy had become the focus of artistic activity. The French king Francis I (reigned 1515–1547) encouraged Italian artists to come to France and work in his court, beginning a new chapter in French art.

In 1515 Francis I conquered the Italian city of Milan. He admired Italian art and was now able to see firsthand altarpieces, frescoes, and sculptures, and to meet some of the artists who had produced them. Of them the most distinguished was Leonardo da Vinci (1452–1519), whom the king invited to settle in France. In 1516 Leonardo went to live near Francis's castle at Amboise. Although Leonardo did not paint any pictures while in France, he delighted the king with his encyclopedic knowledge of art and architecture.

Below: This wall decoration by Rosso Fiorentino in Francis I's palace at Fontainebleau combines paintings with plaster figures. It depicts scenes from classical history and mythology—the elephant at the center is a symbol of royalty.

When Francis I wanted to decorate the Château (palace) of Fontainebleau, a few miles to the southeast of Paris, he turned to two Italian artists, Rosso Fiorentino (1494–1540) and Francesco Primaticcio (1504–1570). Much of their work there was later destroyed, but their masterpiece, the magnificent Francis I Gallery, has survived.

DECORATIONS AT FONTAINEBLEAU

Made between 1534 and 1539, the Francis I Gallery is a long hall lined with wood paneling and decorated with frescoes (wall paintings on "fresh" or wet plaster) and plaster moldings of putti (winged children), garlands of fruit, and nudes. The decorations celebrated the achievements of Francis and the French nation using classical (ancient Greek and Roman) myths and symbols. One of the most famous frescoes is of an elephant (symbolizing royalty) carrying a fleur-de-lis (the iris-shaped symbol of the French kings).

Francis I ordered engravers and tapestry-makers to produce copies of the paintings at Fountainebleau, so that the brilliant new style could be spread throughout France. A style known as the School of Fontainebleau developed, combining the classicism of the Italian Renaissance with a typically French courtly elegance and refinement.

Under the influence of Italian art French artists adopted new subject matter, in particular the nude female body and landscapes with scenes from classical myths. The French-born painter Jean Cousin the Elder (about 1490–1560) painted elegant nudes, influenced by the work of Primaticcio. The Italian-born Niccolò dell' Abbate (about 1512–1571), who lived much of his life in France, produced dreamlike landscapes based on the work of the Italian painter Correggio.

The leading French sculptor of the time was Jean Goujon (about 1510–1568), who was influenced by Benvenuto Cellini, another Italian artist who worked for Francis I. Goujon's masterpiece is the graceful Fountain of the Innocents (1547–1550) in Paris.

During the reign of Henry II one of the most popular subjects for artists was Diana, the Roman goddess of hunting. Depicting her gave artists the opportunity to portray the female nude and to celebrate the beauty of the king's mistress, Diane de Poitiers.

PORTRAITURE

Portraiture was another innovation in French art of the period, although here artists looked to the Flemish painters of northern Europe. Father and son Jean (about 1485–1540) and François (about 1510–1572) Clouet produced intimate, lifelike portraits of the French nobility and royalty, including some magnificent portraits of Francis I.

From 1562 to 1598 France was embroiled in civil war, and the grand tradition of French art revived only with peace, when the new king, Henry IV, commissioned fresh decorations for his palaces. By this time newer styles of art were beginning to arrive from Italy.

Above: This 19th-century painting shows a bustling market square in Paris with the Fountain of the Innocents by Jean Goujon at its center. The sides of the fountain are decorated with sculptures of women pouring water from urns.

SEE ALSO
- Cellini
- Correggio
- Francis I
- Gothic Art
- Leonardo da Vinci
- Mannerism
- Patronage

Galileo

Galileo Galilei (1564–1642) is remembered today mainly for his discoveries in astronomy. But he was also an outstanding mathematician and physicist who carried out pioneering experiments in gravitation and motion, and he is known as the father of modern mechanics.

Galileo was born in Pisa, a town in northwest Italy. Although his father was a musician, the young Galileo had a more scientific turn of mind and decided to study medicine at the University of Pisa. A legend relates how one day while he was in Pisa Cathedral, he watched a lamp swinging. He noted that each swing took the same length of time as all the others no matter how far the lamp swung. That stimulated his interest in mathematics and also led him later in life to suggest that this idea of a pendulum swinging could be used to regulate clocks.

A TEACHER OF MATHEMATICS

In time Galileo's fascination with numbers made him decide to devote himself to mathematics. By the age of 25 he was teaching the subject at the university. In 1592 he moved from Pisa to the University of Padua, in the northeast of Italy, where he remained for the next 18 years. At Padua he carried out many experiments on falling bodies. The ancient Greek philosopher Aristotle had propounded the idea that bodies of different weights fall at different speeds. After measuring the rates of fall of many different objects, Galileo proved that Aristotle

was wrong. His own theory of accelerated motion stated that all falling bodies speed up at the same rate.

In the spring of 1609 Galileo heard about a remarkable new invention—

Galileo discovered that all falling bodies speed up at the same rate

---

the telescope (see box). He built his own, making it much stronger than the original one, so that distant objects were magnified to 33 times the size they appeared to be when viewed with the naked eye. When he observed

Below: An 18th-century wall painting in the Observatory Academy, Florence, showing the young Galileo watching a lamp swinging in Pisa Cathedral. He noticed that each swing of the lamp took the same time as all the others however far the lamp swung, and that gave him the idea of using a swinging pendulum to regulate a clock.

THE TELESCOPE

The telescope is a tubular magnifying instrument that makes distant objects seem much nearer and therefore much larger. It was invented in the early 17th century, probably by a Dutch spectacle-maker named Hans Lippershey, and at first was a relatively simple instrument. It consisted of a tube in which were fitted two glass lenses. The one at the end furthest from the eye was convex, that is, it bulged outward. The one nearest the eye was concave and curved inward. Light passed through the first lens and was focused at the second one, producing an enlarged image of whatever the instrument was pointing at. Galileo developed his own telescope in Venice in 1609, based on the Dutch model. Members of the Venetian senate tested it out and were so impressed by it—not least because it would be useful in warfare—that they rewarded Galileo handsomely.

Above: Galileo presenting his new telescope to the doge of Venice and members of the Venetian senate.

the night sky through his powerful telescope, what he saw contradicted current beliefs about the planets and stars. The moon, for example, was not smooth as had been previously thought but had mountains and valleys, just like the earth. And he was able to see that the planet Jupiter had four moons, or satellites, revolving around it, and that the Milky Way was not just a band of mist but consisted of countless stars.

GALILEO OUTRAGES THE CHURCH

In 1610 Galileo published his findings in a book called *The Starry Messenger*. In it he gave his support to the new Copernican model of the universe, which stated that the sun—not the earth—was at the center of the planetary system. But in doing so he outraged the Catholic church, which upheld the Ptolemaic view that the earth was at the center of the universe. In 1616 Galileo was banned from "holding or defending" Copernicus's

ideas, and he published nothing more for the next 16 years.

However, in 1624 Galiileo obtained permission from the pope to write about the two conflicting world systems—those of Ptolemy and Copernicus—as long as he did it in a noncommittal way. In 1632 he published his *Dialogue of the Two World Systems—Ptolemaic and Copernican*, which, however, made it clear that Galileo supported Copernicus's view of the world. He was summoned to Rome to be formally tried in a church court and was threatened with torture if he did not reject his ideas. After five days of interrogation Galileo agreed to renounce his views. He was sentenced to house arrest.

He spent the remainder of his life on his estate near Florence, where, despite poor health and increasing blindness, he continued to work and produced an important book on mechanics. He died of a fever in January 1642.

SEE ALSO
♦ Astronomy
♦ Copernicus
♦ Padua

Gardens

In the Renaissance period the idea of what a garden should be underwent a radical change. In medieval times gardens were usually small, and their main purpose was for growing herbs to use in medicines and cookery. They were generally enclosed by a wall to create a warm, sheltered spot for the herbs to grow. In Renaissance Italy, however, wealthy noblemen and merchants began building lavish country villas, which had large, elaborately designed gardens with open views that were intended purely as pleasure spots.

The revival of interest during the Renaissance in the art and culture of classical (ancient Greek and Roman) times included an interest in classical gardens. Renaissance architects designed house and garden together, creating a garden that complemented the house. They constructed a formal garden, using plenty of stone, with paths separating geometrical-shaped flowerbeds. Classical features such as statues, grottoes (artificial caves), urns, sundials, temples, pavilions, and fountains were incorporated into the design.

A DISPLAY OF SCULPTURE

One very influential garden was the courtyard garden—called the Belvedere garden—at the Vatican, which was designed by the architect Donato Bramante. It connected the Vatican palace with the Villa Belvedere; and because the ground was uneven, the garden incorporated terraces and steps. The pope's collection of classical antiquities was displayed in the completed garden, so that it seemed like an open-air sculpture gallery.

Above: One of the great Italian gardens at Villa Lante della Rovere near Bagnaia. The extensive formal gardens include an impressive water feature with a central fountain, surrounded by paths and geometrical flowerbeds bounded by low hedges. The grounds are dotted with urns and other sculptural features, plus evergreen shrubs pruned into sculptural shapes.

Gardens increasingly became a matter of fashion and pride to their owners, who strove for ever more elaborate, and ambitious, designs. Gardens were divided into different elements. A parterre garden was a formal garden with beds laid out in a geometric design and separated by graveled walks. It was an area for strolling and conversation, providing peace and tranquillity. Other elements of the Renaissance garden might include a terrace adjoining the house, a paved courtyard garden, a park, or a water garden. Garden layouts ensured that panoramic views and vistas were seen at their best, while in the distance might be glimpsed a "wilderness," a tamed version of wild nature.

Everywhere considerable skill was used to shape the natural landscape. Terracing and stairways solved the problem of sloping land, while rivers and streams were harnessed to provide water features. One of the most famous gardens of Renaissance Italy was built in 1550 at the Villa d'Este at Tivoli, near Rome. The gardens included terraces, walkways, formal beds, ornamental buildings, and fountains—a natural waterway was used to feed the fountains and to power a water organ.

STONEWORK AND SHRUBS

The effect of so much stonework used in these gardens was softened by the lavish planting of evergreen shrubs such as ilex, cypress, laurel, and ivy. The beds in which flowers were grown were divided into decorative geometric compartments edged with neatly trimmed low hedges of herbs such as rosemary or lavender. In the beds grew an increasing number of new flowers brought to Europe from distant lands. Tulips and lilacs from Ottoman Turkey, plus hyacinths, anemones, and cro-

cuses joined the more familiar medieval flowers, such as roses, violets, and marigolds. Plants were carefully chosen for their season of flowering and for their color and perfume. Professional nurseries began to appear to cater to a growing demand for plants, and a class of skilled gardeners developed, adept at pruning and grafting, and knowledgeable about fertilizers and propagation.

The English earl of Leicester's garden at Kenilworth was a typical Renaissance creation. It included a terrace, arbors (shady alcoves formed by trees), alleys, orchards, fountains, statues, concealed waterworks, aviaries, fish ponds, and beautiful flowerbeds, described by a visitor in 1575 as full of "redolent plants and fragrant herbs."

Above: The Ocean Fountain in the Boboli Gardens outside Florence. The fountain was designed by Giambologna (1529–1608), who specialized in garden sculpture.

SEE ALSO
♦ Botany
♦ Classicism
♦ Giambologna
♦ Palaces and Villas

Geneva

The Swiss city of Geneva was destined to play an important role in the history of Protestantism in the mid-16th century, when it became a model Protestant city ruled by the principles of John Calvin.

From the late Middle Ages Geneva had been ruled by its bishop. Although ultimate authority rested in the bishop's hands, the Genevans also governed themselves to some extent. An assembly of citizens consisting of merchants and craftsmen met several times a year. It elected four magistrates and a council of 20 members, who handled the routine affairs of the city.

Since 1416 the bishops had come from the ruling family of the neighboring duchy of Savoy and had tried to strengthen the ties between the duchy and the city. In response the town magistrates looked to the Swiss city of Bern to defend them against Savoy.

When Bern became Protestant in 1525, it had the support of many Genevans, who welcomed any attack on the authority of the Catholic church because of their bitter struggle with the bishop. In 1525 Bern sent troops to Geneva to help the citizens overthrow the current ruler, Pierre de La Baume. The move gave the Protestant church a strong foothold in the city.

Geneva did not become Protestant immediately, however. The city government kept Geneva Catholic until Guillaume Farel (1489–1565) arrived

Below: A view of the city of Geneva today across Lake Geneva—the city is set at the southwest corner of the lake where the Rhône River flows out of it. Geneva gained particular importance in the 16th century as a center of Protestantism.

in 1533. Farel was a follower of Huldrych Zwingli, a leading Protestant intellectual from Zurich. Farel was expelled, but he returned, and his persistence paid off when the council organized a debate between him and his followers and two Catholic clergymen in 1535. The council ruled in favor of the Protestant side and imposed Protestant services on the city.

The Catholic duke of Savoy refused to accept the Genevans' decision and soon laid siege to the city. Once more the Genevans were forced to turn to Bern for military support. After the armies of Savoy had been defeated, Geneva officially became Protestant. In 1536 the assembly of citizens voted to endorse the teaching of Protestant doctrine and to expel the Catholic clergy from the city.

JOHN CALVIN

In the same year that Geneva became Protestant, the young French religious thinker John Calvin (1509–1564) stopped in the city in the middle of a journey to Strasbourg. Farel knew of him because of the publication earlier that year of Calvin's religious text *Institutes of the Christian Religion.* He begged him to stay and turn Geneva into a truly reformed city. Calvin reluctantly agreed and quickly emerged as the major authority in the Church of Geneva. However, theɪe were many people in the city who were still loyal to the Catholic faith, and Calvin and Farel made many enemies who were unwilling to accept their beliefs. In 1538 they were expelled.

Three years later Calvin's allies regained power in Geneva and invited him to come back to the city. Calvin's price for returning was that the city council allow him to reorganize the church and supervise the religious

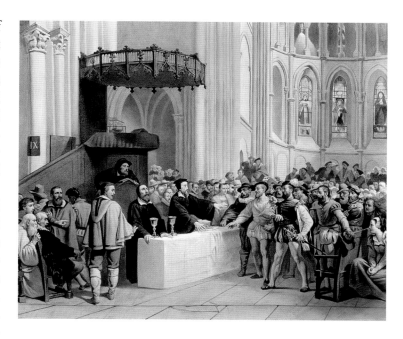

education of its citizens. Calvin dominated Geneva from 1541 until his death in 1564. In 1559 he founded the Academy of Geneva to train pastors to spread his beliefs across Europe. The city soon became the center of Protestantism. The Scottish religious leader John Knox later called it the "truest city of God on earth."

PROTESTANT REFUGE

Largely because of Calvin's presence in Geneva the city became a center of refuge for Protestants from France and Italy. Many of them were very wealthy, and their families increasingly gained political power in the city. Local resentment toward the outsiders led to an unsuccessful revolt in 1555. It was the last internal attempt to overthrow the Calvinist domination of the city. However, the city of Geneva continued to be threatened by Savoy, which made several attempts to regain control of it until one final effort proved unsuccessful in 1602. Geneva's alliance with the Swiss Confederation prevented any attacks on the city by the Catholic powers Spain and France.

Above: This 19th-century painting shows John Calvin in Saint Peter's Cathedral, Geneva, refusing Holy Communion to a group of men because of their immoral behavior. Calvin's rule banned many activities such as drinking, gambling, and dancing.

SEE ALSO

♦ Calvin
♦ Luther
♦ Protestantism
♦ Reformation
♦ Zwingli

Genoa

The city of Genoa, on the northwest coast of Italy, was an important port in the Middle Ages and the center of a vast trading network. Originally an ancient fishing village, the developing city supplied many of the ships and much of the equipment needed to take Christian Crusaders to the Holy Land in the 12th and 13th centuries. As Genoa grew, it established trading colonies all around the Mediterranean and also took control of the surrounding countryside in the coastal region of

Above: The harbor of Genoa as it appeared in the late 16th century. By this time the city had been an important European port for several centuries.

Liguria, as well as parts of the islands of Corsica and Sardinia. The height of Genoese power came in the late 13th century, when the city defeated two important naval rivals in battle—Pisa and Venice.

Even though Genoa was flourishing economically, the city was being torn apart by struggles between rival political factions. In 1339 the Genoese tried to bring an end to the strife by appointing a doge (or chief magistrate) to rule the city. This arrangement had

SAINT CATHERINE OF GENOA

Catherine of Genoa (1447–1510) was born into a noble Genoese family—the Fieschi. Her early education led her to wish to become a nun, but instead her family arranged for her to marry Giuliano Adorno, a young Genoese nobleman. Catherine's marriage was generally an unhappy one. However, in 1473 her life was transformed when she experienced a vision. From this point onward she dedicated herself to helping the sick and poor people of Genoa. In particular she worked at the hospital of Pammatane. As a result of her work with the sick, Catherine caught the plague. Although she survived the disease, she suffered from ill health for much of the rest of her life. She died in 1510, leaving behind two works, *Dialogues on the Soul and the Body* and *Treatise on Purgatory*. She was made a saint in 1737.

proved to be very successful in Venice. However, the move did little to make Genoa more stable. It was constantly at war with Venice and in 1380 lost a crucial naval battle against its rival at Chioggia. From this point the power and influence of Genoa declined considerably. The city fell to French forces in 1394 and spent much of the 15th century under the control of either France or Milan.

ANDREA DORIA

It was not until the early 16th century that the fortunes of Genoa revived. In 1522 the city was taken by forces of the king of Spain and Holy Roman emperor Charles V. Five years later the mercenary soldier Andrea Doria (1466–1560) recaptured the city on behalf of King Francis I of France. Doria was a member of a noble family that had played a major role in Genoese politics for centuries. Angry with the way he was being treated by Francis, Doria changed his allegiance to Charles V in 1528. In September of that year he drove the French back out of the city. As a reward the emperor allowed him to rule Genoa on his behalf.

In 1528 Doria introduced a new constitution to the republic, which from then on was run by a council

Left: This 16th-century portrait of the admiral and ruler of Genoa Andrea Doria depicts him as the Roman sea god Neptune, a reference to the many great naval victories that he won.

made up of members of the important families of noble Genoese merchants. However, Doria himself exerted a considerable influence on the running of the city. By doing so, he managed to stabilize Genoa and rid it of the infighting that had plagued it for centuries. Under Doria's rule many great artists were attracted to the city. Among the most important was the architect Galeazzo Alessi, who designed a number of Genoa's most beautiful buildings. Genoa continued to flourish after Doria's death in 1560, benefiting economically from its close relationship with Spain.

SEE ALSO
- Charles V
- City-States
- Constantinople
- Francis I
- Holy Roman Empire
- Italy
- Trade
- Venice

Gentileschi

Artemisia Gentileschi (about 1593–1652) was one of the first great female artists. Her powerful, dramatic style was typical of the baroque era. Born in Rome, Artemisia was the daughter of the well-known painter Orazio Gentileschi, who taught her drawing and painting. In 1612 Orazio arranged a marriage for Artemisia to the Florentine painter Pietro di Stiattesi. They had four children before separating around 1624.

Artemisia then moved to Venice. By 1638 she was living at the court of the English king Charles I, where she assisted her father in painting the ceiling of the Queen's House at Greenwich. After Orazio's death she returned to Italy to live in Naples, where she died around 1652.

Like her father, Artemisia was a follower of the baroque painter Caravaggio. She completed her first masterpiece, *Susanna and the Elders*, in 1611. Her father tirelessly promoted her work to wealthy art collectors, some of whom became lifelong patrons. Orazio also helped Artemisia become the first woman admitted to the Florentine Accademia del Disegno, or Academy of Design, in 1616.

DRAMATIC SCENES

Known for her dramatic scenes of classical and biblical stories using realistic figures and intense lighting, Artemisia received commissions from many powerful patrons throughout her career. In particular, she specialized in painting heroic women, such as Susanna, Lucretia, and Cleopatra. One of her most famous pieces of work is *Judith and Holofernes* (about 1620). It illustrates a story from the Old Testament in which the Jewish heroine Judith beheads a Syrian general. Artemisia also painted several self-portraits, including the *Self-Portrait as the Allegory of Painting* (1630). Her letters to her patrons show both her pride and her determination to win international renown. One of the very few successful women artists of the 17th century, Gentileschi had a lasting influence on later baroque painters.

Above: **Judith and Holofernes,** *painted in about 1620, is one of Gentileschi's most famous, and powerful, paintings.*

SEE ALSO
♦ Baroque
♦ Painting
♦ Women

German Art

Left: Grünewald's
Isenheim Altarpiece
(about 1515) is one
of the best-known
German paintings
of the Renaissance.
It is a powerful
depiction of Christ's
suffering—his body
is thin and twisted,
his flesh is torn
with cuts and
thorns, and blood
pours from wounds
in his side and feet.

In the Renaissance Germany
was not a single, well-defined
country but a collection of about 300
different states. Most were subject to
the Holy Roman emperor but in
practice were ruled by local princes or
bishops, or were self-governing city-
states. The art produced in these lands
varied a great deal, although there
were similarities. The influence of the
Gothic style that dominated medieval
art meant that many German artists
continued to use elongated figures
and clothing with deeply modeled
folds. They produced real-looking,
often dramatic, images far from the
idealized beauty of Italian art.

There were regional variations in the
art produced in the area now known as
Germany. In the northwest, on the
border with Flanders (present-day Belgium and parts of the Netherlands and
northern France), art was influenced
by the close observation of everyday
appearances typical of Flemish painting. Artists in the south, however, were
more influenced by Italian art, and
began to paint the nude human body
and subjects from ancient Greek and
Roman myths. Germany's position at
the heart of Europe and the major
trade routes that ran through its lands
also made German artists receptive to
influences from other countries.

ART AND THE REFORMATION

Many German artists in the 16th century were affected by the turmoil of the Reformation. This religious movement began as an attempt to combat abuses in the Roman Catholic church and resulted in the formation of the Protestant church, which broke away from the authority of the pope. Eventually, the Reformation divided Germany, with the south remaining largely Catholic and the north becoming mainly Protestant.

One painter who was affected by the upheaval was Matthias Grünewald. He was sympathetic to Martin Luther, who spearheaded the Protestant cause, and he lost his post as court painter to Archbishop Albrecht of Mainz after the Peasants' War of 1524–1525. This unsuccessful revolt was partly inspired by Luther's teaching, and in one of the clashes the archbishop was almost killed. Another German painter, Jörg Ratgeb, was executed in 1526 for his part in the revolt.

In the Catholic south the church continued to commission architecture, sculpture, and painting, and the arts flourished. However, in the north the Protestants were opposed to religious images, and they destroyed countless paintings and sculptures, and commissioned little new work from artists.

Despite these outside influences, German art retained its own distinctive characteristics, notably its powerful expression of emotions. This quality can be seen most clearly in the paintings of Matthias Grünewald (about 1460–1528), particularly the *Isenheim Altarpiece* that he completed in about 1515 (shown on page 41). This painting was made to go behind an altar in a hospital chapel, and it was intended to show the terrible suffering of Christ, no doubt to reassure the patients who saw it that they were not alone in their suffering. Unlike Italian painters, who idealized Christ and made his body beautiful, Grünewald exaggerated the horror and pain of his death. Christ's flesh is a deathly color, covered in thorns and weeping wounds; blood pours from his twisted feet where they are nailed to the cross; and his head hangs down.

DÜRER AND HOLBEIN

The two other leading German artists of the early 16th century were Albrecht Dürer (1471–1528) and Hans Holbein the Younger (about 1497–1543). Together with Grünewald they covered a wide range of artistic expression.

Grünewald painted only religious scenes, and he belongs essentially to the mystical spiritual world of the Middle Ages. Dürer, in contrast, was a man of the Renaissance, with a ceaselessly inquiring mind. He was always ready to try new subjects, approaches, and techniques, and he twice visited Italy to increase his knowledge of the latest developments in art. Although he worked ceaselessly to incorporate ideas

Right: Altdorfer's **Saint George and the Dragon,** *a painting that shows the important part played by landscape in his work. The scene of Saint George slaying the dragon is almost an incidental detail amid the delicate trees of the forest.*

from Italian art into his own work, his prints and paintings retained the directness that is evident in Grünewald's work and that characterizes German art in general. He painted the world as it was, showing ugliness as well as beauty.

Holbein too was a versatile artist, but he is famous above all as an

---

Dürer painted the world as it was, showing ugliness as well as beauty

---

exceptional portrait painter. His portraits combine the grandeur and authority of Italian art with the minute detail typical of Flemish and German art. It is uncertain whether Holbein ever visited Italy, but he spent most of his career outside Germany, first in neighboring Switzerland, then in England, where he was court painter to King Henry VIII. His portrait of Henry VIII has become the best-known image of the great Tudor monarch.

There were many other illustrious German painters in this period, among them Albrecht Altdorfer (about 1485–1538) and Lucas Cranach the Elder (1472–1553). Altdorfer is best known for pictures showing scenes from Bible stories that are set in beautiful landscapes. He was probably the first European artist to paint a "pure" landscape—that is, a picture that shows nature for itself and includes no human figures. Early in his career Cranach also painted intricate religious scenes set in landscapes, as well as some fine portraits, and he later specialized in paintings based on classical myths.

Germany also boasted some outstanding sculptors, and the two greatest were Tilman Riemenschneider (about 1460–1531) and Veit Stoss (about 1438–1533). They specialized in wood-carving, using wood from the common lime, or linden, tree. Their work is Gothic rather than Renaissance in spirit and is carved with an intensity of feeling similar to that of Grünewald's paintings. Stoss and Riemenschneider often produced their carvings for altarpieces, representing holy figures and Bible stories using elegant, slim figures, with deeply cut, expressive clothing. Some of their sculptures were gilded (covered with gold) and painted, a common practice in medieval art, although their later work was often left plain, reflecting the Renaissance trend away from elaborate imagery.

Above: A scene of the Last Supper in the **Holy Blood Altarpiece** *(about 1499–1505), carved from limewood by Riemenschneider.*

SEE ALSO

♦ Dürer
♦ Flemish Painting
♦ Germany
♦ Gothic Art
♦ Henry VIII
♦ Holbein
♦ Landscape Painting
♦ Portraiture
♦ Reformation
♦ Sculpture

Germany

For centuries Germany was not a single state but a very loose grouping of hundreds of princely and other territories inhabited by German-speaking peoples. In the 15th century many of the German cities became free cities, fragmenting power even more, and in the 16th century the Protestant Reformation created further divisions that would affect the history of Germany for hundreds of years.

The nearest thing to a German state was the Holy Roman Empire. Most of the people living within the empire were Germans, but not all of them. The Czech kingdom of Bohemia, for example, was an important part of the empire, and it was Slavic-speaking. There were also German-speaking people living beyond the borders of the empire, particularly in the lands to the northeast around the Baltic Sea. These lands were settled by German peasants and townspeople, and were controlled by the Teutonic Order, which had originally consisted of crusaders called the "Teutonic Knights." By about 1500 German-speaking people were becoming conscious of themselves as a separate nation, although—unlike the French, English, or Hungarians—they did not have their own nation-state.

DIVISIONS WITHIN THE EMPIRE

The Holy Roman Empire did have an emperor at its head, but his power was very limited. The empire consisted of hundreds of more or less independent territories, including principalities, free cities, and the smaller territories of lesser nobles or knights. That made it hard to maintain law and order, especially since the knights were a declining class who quite often behaved like robber barons. The more powerful princes ruled areas, such as Bavaria, Württemberg, Hesse, Saxony, and Brandenburg, that were potentially independent states. There were also ecclesiastical princes—churchmen such as the "prince-bishops" of Mainz, Trier, and Cologne—who controlled wide areas.

Above: The Holy Roman emperor Maximilian I. The emperor supposedly ruled over a huge area of central Europe, including all of present-day Germany, but many regional rulers were effectively independent.

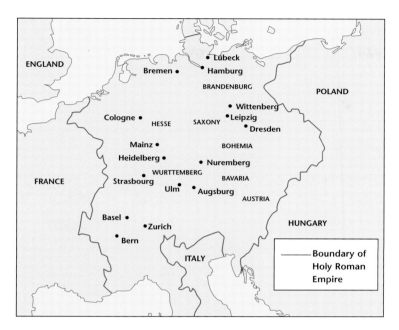

Above: A map showing some of the chief cities and regions of Germany in the 15th and 16th centuries.

Despite the political confusion, Germany at the beginning of the Renaissance period was becoming wealthier, and its population was increasing. In the 14th century the German people, along with all other Europeans, had suffered from the devastating plague called the Black Death, and the population had fallen

---

At the beginning of the Renaissance period Germany was becoming wealthier

---

by a third or more. A gradual recovery began in the early 15th century, and by 1500 the population of Germany had returned to preplague levels.

Prosperity was most evident in the towns. There were a great many of them, although most of them were quite small—only Cologne and Augsburg had more than 40,000 inhabitants. Germany's central position in Europe meant that its cities

were on the main trade routes, which initially were not seriously affected by the discovery of America in 1492 and of a new sea route to Asia in 1499. From the 13th century a league of north German towns—the Hanseatic League—had dominated the trade in herring, timber, and grain around the Baltic Sea. Cologne benefited from east–west commerce and traffic down the Rhine River, while the southern cities of Augsburg and Nuremberg controlled the trade routes across the Alps to Italy and the Mediterranean Sea.

SILVER AND SALT

Industrial production in Germany was on a small scale, but was nevertheless significant. Lüneburg, one of the Hanseatic towns, was a major producer of salt, which was extracted from its brine springs. Mining and the related industry of metalworking were more widespread. Coal, iron, copper, and

THE HANSEATIC LEAGUE

In the Renaissance period trade in Germany was dominated by the activities of the Hanseatic League, which was a confederation of towns and cities that were based largely around the Baltic Sea. The league had been formed in the mid-13th century when flourishing trading towns such as Lübeck and Hamburg had come to an agreement to act together to defend themselves against pirates, keep out competitors, and resist interference by foreign rulers when they traded abroad. The league took its name from the German word *hanse*, which means a guild or association.

By the beginning of the 15th century the league numbered over 100 cities. Other important cities included Bremen, Cologne, and Visby on the Swedish island of Gotland in the Baltic Sea. The league maintained bases with special privileges in many other towns, from York in England to Novgorod in Russia. Its main trading goods were wool from Flanders, fish from Sweden, and timber and furs from Russia. The Hanseatic League remained active throughout the 15th and 16th centuries, although it gradually became less dominant.

A FOOL'S PARADISE

The most popular German literary work of the Renaissance period was a satire entitled *The Ship of Fools*, written by the poet Sebastian Brant (about 1458–1521). Born in Strasbourg, Brant was a court official to the Holy Roman emperor Maximilian I. In *The Ship of Fools* the vessel of the title sets sail for Narragonia, the "fool's paradise." The journey allows Brant to introduce a multitude of characters, each one representing a different sin or shortcoming. Drunkards, misers, and busybodies are all attacked, as are the clergy, who are portrayed as greedy, corrupt, and lecherous. In part, the work was intended as a call to reform the church. However, few sections of German society escaped unscathed.

First published in 1494, Brant's work quickly became extremely popular. It is significant that it was written in German rather than Latin, which meant that many ordinary people could read and understand it, and this undoubtedly added to its success. The book's illustrations are believed to be by Brant's compatriot, the artist Albrecht Dürer. Later it also provided the inspiration for a work by Hieronymus Bosch.

silver were mined, providing the raw materials for the manufacture of armaments and armor, a specialty of Augsburg. Made into silver coins, German silver helped power the

Below: Merchants meet at the quayside in the wealthy port of Hamburg.

European economy until the mid-16th century, when the metal began to flood in from mines in the New World. Investment in the silver mines of the Tyrol made the fortunes of two great banking houses—the Fuggers and the Welsers—whose loans influenced international politics.

The increase in population that occurred in the 15th century meant there was a greater demand for food, and that encouraged farmers to produce more. But in many places the

---

In response to inflation landlords demanded higher payments from the peasants

---

condition of the peasants became worse. One reason was that expanding trade and the production of silver caused inflation (a general rise in prices). Landlords responded by demanding larger payments from the peasants. In the west the peasants' lot became much harder; in the east, where large grain-growing estates were being set up, they were reduced to serfdom (which meant that they were not allowed to leave the land and were virtually slaves to their masters). As a result there was considerable peasant unrest all through the 15th century and into the next. Many landlords were clergymen, and tenant anger became mixed with a more general feeling of resentment against church figures, who were seen as being greedy, corrupt, and uninterested in spiritual issues. This feeling eventually helped fuel the Protestant Reformation.

PRINTING AND CULTURE

It was in Germany that the greatest European innovation of the 15th century took place—printing with movable type. It first appeared in the 1440s and 1450s, and soon crossed the Alps into Italy. Civil servants and scholars educated in the manner of Renaissance humanists also thrived in German cities. Thanks to printing, their works quickly became known to many readers, particularly in the towns, where about 30 percent of the citizens are thought to have been able to read. Artists also began to be influenced by the new ideas of Renaissance Italy. A leading German artist was Albrecht Dürer (1471–1528), who studied in Italy at the end of the 15th century and returned to Germany to become an outstanding printmaker and painter in oils. Other important German artists of the early 16th century included Matthias Grünewald and Hans Holbein the Younger.

THE PEASANTS' REVOLT

Above: This engraving shows Thomas Müntzer (left, standing) preaching to his followers shortly before the battle of Frankenhausen. Müntzer believed that the poor were closer to God than the rich and urged them to revolt against their rulers.

In June 1524 Germany's peasants rose in open revolt against high taxes and the burden of labor services. The movement started in the Black Forest and quickly spread to other parts of Germany. Some of those who took part were well-off peasants who resented the way that princes and landlords were gradually taking away their rights. The rebels were also inspired by the revolutionary new religious ideas introduced by Martin Luther and other reformers, and claimed the right to elect their own priests. Luther, however, was outraged by their stand and urged the princes to slaughter the rebels without mercy.

Greatly alarmed, the princes and the upper classes struck back savagely. Without military experience, the peasants were routed at one battle after another. Despite these defeats, the revolts continued, and a visionary named Thomas Müntzer emerged as a leader, proclaiming that the Second Coming of Christ on Earth was about to happen. In May 1525 at the battle of Frankenhausen the rebel forces were routed, and 5,000 peasants were slain. Müntzer was taken prisoner, tortured, and executed. It was the end of the Peasants' Revolt.

Right: The reformer Martin Luther (far left) appears before the Holy Roman emperor Charles V (seated) at the Diet of Worms in 1521. The assembly required Luther to retract his heretical beliefs, but he refused to do so. Shortly afterward he was banned from the church.

In the early 16th century the Catholic church was particularly unpopular in Germany, where there was great resistance to paying taxes to the papacy, which was seen as a foreign institution. This discontent with the church culminated in the Protestant Reformation, which was begun by Martin Luther in 1517. The Reformation was a decisive event in Germany's history. It divided the country between Catholics and Protestants, with Protestantism at its strongest in the north. Protestant humanist scholars promoted writing in the German language, as opposed to Latin, the international scholarly language. Luther's translation of the Bible into German had an enormous influence on the development and use of the German language.

THE PEACE OF AUGSBURG

The Reformation was to have an enduring effect on Germany's history. Although the Holy Roman emperor Charles V (ruled 1519–1556) made a determined attempt to assert his imperial authority and stamp out Protestantism, he failed dismally. The German princes, whether they were Protestant or Catholic, had no wish to

> *The German princes had no wish to yield power to the emperor*

yield any of their power to the emperor. The Peace of Augsburg (1555) gave the princes the right to decide the religion of their subjects—and it became clear that Germany would remain fragmented, with each prince virtually an independent ruler. Consequently, when religious passions flared up again in the 17th century, a divided Germany became the battleground of foreign powers and ended in ruins. There was to be no unified Germany until late in the 19th century.

Ghiberti

Lorenzo Ghiberti (1378–1455) was a leading sculptor in Florence at the beginning of the 15th century. His most important works are two sets of sculpted bronze doors made for the baptistery of Florence Cathedral, which are among the greatest achievements of the early Renaissance. Ghiberti's work had a refined, elegant style that reflected his training as a goldsmith and drew on the sophisticated, decorative style popular in art of the time, called the International Gothic. These influences were combined with an interest in classical (ancient Greek and Roman) art to create some of the most lyrical sculptures of the period.

Ghiberti grew up in Florence in the house of his mother's second husband, Bartolo di Michele, who may also have been Ghiberti's father (it is not clear which of his mother's husbands was Ghiberti's father). Bartolo was a goldsmith, and Ghiberti trained in his workshop before leaving the city briefly to work as a painter. He returned in 1400 when a prestigious competition was announced to find an artist to design a set of bronze doors for the baptistery of Florence Cathedral. Seven artists entered; each of them had to submit a bronze panel ilustrating the sacrifice of Isaac, a subject from the Old Testament.

WINNING DESIGN
In 1403 Ghiberti was announced as the winner, narrowly beating the more experienced artist Brunelleschi (1377–1446). The winning panel featured a design in relief—that is, the sculpted figures stood out from a flat background. It is likely that the judges were influenced by both the artistic qualities and the financial advantages of Ghiberti's entry. Compared to Brunelleschi's panel, Ghiberti's has a harmonious design, with all the figures of the story fitted together effortlessly in a rocky landscape. Their flowing clothes are gathered in folds and edged with delicate patterns, while the naked body of Isaac reflects the ideal beauty of classical sculptures. Ghiberti's tech-

Below: Ghiberti's Sacrifice of Isaac (1401), the panel with which he won the competition to design the baptistery doors for Florence Cathedral. It shows an Old Testament scene in which Abraham is about to sacrifice his son Isaac to prove his devotion to God.

Above: The Doors of Paradise (1425–1452), Ghiberti's second set of doors for the baptistery of Florence Cathedral.

produce the panels, Ghiberti ran a large workshop. Many important artists received their training there, including Donatello and Uccello.

DOORS OF PARADISE

By 1424 the doors were finished and were such a success that Ghiberti was commissioned to produce another set. This time there were only 10 panels, and they were set in square frames, allowing Ghiberti more space and freedom in his designs. The subjects were chosen by Leonardo Bruni, a leading Florentine scholar, and showed scenes from the Old Testament. These panels are even more lyrical than those for Ghiberti's first set of doors. They are sculpted in very shallow relief so that the figures stand out only a little way and appear to melt away into the background. These doors soon became known as the "Doors of Paradise."

INFLUENCES AND IDEAS

Ghiberti was much influenced by Donatello's low-relief carvings, and his work also mirrors other new developments in art, particularly the ideas of Leon Battista Alberti. Alberti had written about painting and sculpture, and how the rules of ancient Greek and Roman architecture could be applied to modern buildings. Ghiberti used the forms of classical architecture to create suitable settings for his subjects and to display the newly developed system of perspective, which enabled artists to create a realistic sense of space in their pictures. Like Alberti, Ghiberti felt that all art should be based on the study of classical examples. Toward the end of his life he summed up his ideas in *I Commentarii* ("Commentaries"), three books about classical art, recent art (which included his autobiography), and theory.

nical skill also impressed the judges. He cast his panel hollow, so using much less bronze than the solid panel made by Brunelleschi.

The subject of the baptistery doors is the life of Christ, which Ghiberti depicted in 20 panels, with eight panels underneath portraying heads of the evangelists and church fathers. Each panel is set in a shape called a quatrefoil—a four-part shape that was popular in Gothic art and had been used to frame the panels of an earlier set of doors made for the baptistery by the sculptor Andrea Pisano. The design, modeling, casting, finishing, and gilding of each panel involved a great deal of work, and to help him

Giambologna

Giambologna (1529–1608) was one of the most successful sculptors working in Florence in the 16th century, second only in fame to Michelangelo. His work ranged from large monumental sculptures to small bronze statuettes, all characterized by their refined style and often highly complex arrangements, features typical of the mannerist style. Giambologna's patrons included many heads of state, and his work was avidly collected throughout Europe.

Giambologna was born in Douai, which was then in the Spanish Netherlands and is now in northern France. He trained with the local sculptor Jacques Dubroeucq before going to Rome in 1555 to complete his studies. It was while in Italy that he became known as Giambologna. His original name was Jean Boulogne, which the Italians "translated" as Giovanni Bologna and then shortened to Giambologna. He spent two years in Rome, where he was influenced by classical (ancient Greek and Roman) sculpture and the work of Michelangelo.

Giambologna moved to Florence in about 1557. There he soon attracted the patronage of the powerful Medici family and made his name with a series of large monumental sculptures. They included works carved from marble such as his dramatic *Samson Slaying a Philistine* (1560–1562), in which the figures are interlocked in complex poses, reflecting the influence of the *Laocoön*, a classical (ancient Greek) sculpture that was greatly admired in the Renaissance. Giambologna also created a majestic bronze statue of Cosimo de Medici (1587–1593) riding a horse, which was widely imitated by other sculptors.

As well as producing monumental works, Giambologna also specialized in making garden sculpture. He sculpted fountains and statues for the famous Boboli Gardens just outside Florence, and in the gardens of a Medici palace in Pratolino he also made a huge crouching giant, which was big enough to contain a couple of rooms.

STATUE OF MERCURY

Although many of Giambologna's statues consisted of several figures combined in complicated poses, his most famous work is a bronze sculpture of a single figure: *Flying Mercury* (1580). It shows Mercury, messenger of the gods, poised elegantly on one foot. Giambologna succeeded in creating the sense of Mercury's movement by making his smooth, lithe body twist and stretch upward. The sculpture appears to be almost weightless, with only Mercury's left foot resting on the ground.

The sculpture was originally made as a fountain for the Villa Medici in Rome and was soon copied in many small-scale, bronze statuettes made both in Giambologna's own workshop and elsewhere. Because they were easy to transport, statuettes such as these helped spread the sculptor's fame throughout Europe.

Below: The bronze statue of the Roman god Mercury, one of Giambologna's best-known works.

SEE ALSO
♦ Gardens
♦ Mannerism
♦ Sculpture

Giorgione

Giorgione (about 1477–1510) was an influential painter who inspired a golden age of painting in the north Italian city of Venice. He introduced an atmospheric feeling to his pictures and new types of subject to appeal to learned collectors. Although Giorgione died young and few of his paintings survive, other painters, notably Titian, imitated and developed his style.

Very little is known about Giorgione's life. His real name was Giorgio Barbarelli—Giorgione means "big George," a nickname that suggests he was large or tall—and he came from Castelfranco del Veneto, near Venice. He almost certainly studied under Giovanni Bellini, the leading Venetian painter at the time, since his paintings are very close to Bellini's later work in technique, color, and mood. He died aged 33, probably from the plague.

Giorgione's best-known work is *The Tempest* (about 1505). In this picture Giorgione gave landscape a new prominence and filled the scene with a dreamlike mood. Earlier artists had used landscape only as a background, but Giorgione gave it as much importance as the people. He also filled his picture with atmosphere, capturing the sense of an impending storm by bathing the scene in unearthly light.

The Tempest has an added air of mystery because today it is not known who the elegant young man and the mother and child are. It is likely that they are characters from a classical (ancient Greek or Roman) story. This

type of "pastoral" scene, showing figures relaxing in an idyllic landscape, became popular in the Renaissance.

A similar poetic mood fills *Sleeping Venus* (about 1510), a picture finished by Titian after Giorgione's death. It shows the goddess Venus lying asleep in an idyllic landscape, her nude body pale and slightly elongated to make her more beautiful. This subject was taken up by later Renaissance painters who used it as a way of showing the beauty of the female body. Giorgione brought the same subtlety and restraint to portraiture, and pictures such as his serene *Portrait of a Young Man* (about 1504) influenced many later artists.

Above: Giorgione gave landscape and atmosphere a new importance in The Tempest, *painted in about 1505.*

SEE ALSO

♦ Bellini, Giovanni
♦ Human Form in Art
♦ Landscape Painting
♦ Portraiture
♦ Titian

Giotto

Giotto di Bondone (about 1266–1337) was an Italian painter whom scholars traditionally regard as the father of the Renaissance. Giorgio Vasari, a 16th-century painter and art historian, wrote that Giotto "alone succeeded in resuscitating art and restoring her to a path that may be called the true one." Giotto was the first artist to move away from the stiff, stylized manner of medieval painting. In his pictures people look more realistic and three dimensional, and scenes have more passion and drama.

Although Giotto was famous in his own lifetime, few documents about

him or his work survive. He was born near Florence, probably the son of a peasant. Scholars believe that he was trained by the Italian painter Cimabue (about 1240–1302), who also tried to break free from the medieval style.

Giotto worked in Rome and Padua before buying a house in Florence in 1305. He was probably based in the city from this time, though from 1329 to 1333 he worked in Naples as court painter to Robert of Anjou. In 1334 he was appointed chief architect at Florence Cathedral, where he designed the bell tower. This was a prestigious appointment and reflected the great esteem in which he was held. Giotto's

Above: **The Raising of Lazarus,** *one of the scenes from the life of Christ that Giotto painted in the Arena Chapel in Padua. Giotto reduced the picture to its bare essentials and concentrated on the human drama as Christ brings Lazarus back to life.*

renown was itself a new development. In the medieval period it was unusual for artists to attract any sort of fame.

Scholars have attributed several major works to Giotto, though there is still some debate as to whether he painted them. Most are frescoes, that is, wall paintings made on "fresh" (or wet) plaster. They include a series of paintings showing the life of Saint Francis in the church of San Francesco in Assisi (about 1297–1305) and frescoes in the church of Santa Croce in Florence thought to have been painted in the 1320s and 1330s. The only major work that has always been accepted as Giotto's is a remarkable series of frescoes covering the walls of the Arena Chapel in Padua (1305–1308).

PAINTINGS IN THE ARENA CHAPEL

The Arena Chapel was commissioned by the wealthy Scrovegni family in 1303 and takes its name from the site of the Roman amphitheater, or arena, on which it was built. Giotto decorated the chapel with pictures arranged in three tiers. They show scenes from the lives of Joachim and Anna (the Virgin Mary's parents) and scenes from the lives of Mary and Christ. Below these three tiers Giotto painted figures representing Christian virtues and vices. He painted them in shades of gray to look like statues, a technique known as grisaille. They are the earliest examples of this type of painting in Italian art. A painting of the Last Judgment fills the west wall.

A NEW APPROACH TO PAINTING

Giotto brought a new approach to all these scenes. Compared to other artists of the time, he made his pictures more real-looking and emotionally involving. He set the Bible stories he painted against simplified landscapes rather than the flat gold backgrounds that were common in medieval paintings. He created a sense of space in his pictures and also drew people in scale with one another—medieval artists often made them different sizes. His figures are more weighty and solid than those of his contemporaries. Giotto thought about each scene and figure afresh. He stripped away unnecessary details and expressed the drama of the stories through the gestures and faces of the people he painted.

The scene showing the raising of Lazarus is typical of Giotto's style. It depicts Jesus bringing Lazarus back from the dead. Wrapped in a funeral cloth, Lazarus emerges from his rock-cut tomb. Jesus faces him, raising his hand in greeting, his face full of concentration. The onlookers stare either at Lazarus or at Jesus, and some hold up their hands in amazement. Their faces express strong emotion. Giotto manages to make the characters come alive, and he makes the viewer feel involved in the drama.

Glass

Glass has been produced since ancient times. It is made by heating silica, which is found in sand and quartz, to an extremely high temperature. The silica melts and cools to form a hard—but fragile—water-resistant, transparent material. These qualities mean that glass has long been used to make drinking vessels, containers, and windows. In the Renaissance the northern Italian city of Venice led the world in glassmaking, producing vessels that were sought after in courts and wealthy households across Europe.

For most of the Middle Ages only very basic glass objects—such as beakers made from green or brown glass—were produced in western Europe. Islamic countries like Egypt, Iran, and Syria were the major centers of luxury glassmaking, producing elaborately shaped and decorated vessels.

However, from the 13th century craftsmen in France, England, and Germany began to produce large windows made from pieces of stained (colored) glass to decorate cathedrals. Also, for the first time since the decline of the Roman Empire plain glass began to be used in house windows—although only the wealthiest members of society could afford such a luxury. It was also at this time that glassmaking became a major industry in Venice.

GLASSMAKING IN VENICE

By the 15th century Venice had overtaken Islamic countries as the major producer of luxury glass objects.

Glassmaking began in Venice in the seventh century. By 1291 it had grown to such an extent that the Venetian government moved all the glassmakers to Murano, an island away from the main city, to reduce the risk of fire damage from their kilns. The Venetian government regulated the industry with strict laws to ensure the quality of its products. It also forbade glassmakers from leaving the city or revealing their secrets to outsiders.

Left: A 15th-century Italian chalice used to hold sacred wine during the Communion service. The chalice is made from blue glass with enameled decoration showing the flight into Egypt, when Mary and Joseph fled to Egypt with the baby Jesus to escape from King Herod.

Above: An elaborate glass pitcher made in the shape of a ship. Highly decorated forms like this are typical of Renaissance Venetian glassware.

SEE ALSO

♦ Decorative Arts
♦ Gothic Art
♦ Venice

together differently colored threads of glass to form a rod. This was cut crossways to make multicolored circles that were incorporated in the finished piece.

The Venetians also developed a technique called enameling. Enamel is a soft glass colored with metal oxides that is applied as a powder or paste to the surfaces of glass vessels (it was also used to decorate metal objects) and heated to a high temperature to make it hard. Although enameled glassware had been made before, its secret had been lost until the Venetian glassmaker Angelo Barovier rediscovered it.

Enameled glassware was often richly colored in blue, green, or purple, and featured designs popular in painting and ceramics—such as portraits, coats of arms, grotesques (fanciful combinations of human and animals), and allegories (symbolic stories)—as well as more abstract patterns. By the mid-16th century a complex type of decoration called *latticinio* had also become popular, which involved twisting threads of white glass inside clear glass to create a latticework effect.

CRYSTAL GLASS

During the 14th and 15th centuries glassmakers across Europe tried and failed to copy the closely guarded Venetian designs. However, the demand and rewards were so great that by the 16th century some skilled glassmakers did leave Venice for other countries, where they developed *façon de Venise*, or "Venetian-style glass." By the mid-17th century Venetian glassmaking declined due to competition from countries like England. There, glassmakers developed a crystal glass that was easier to cut (glass was often decorated with designs cut into its surface), more transparent, and more durable than Venetian *cristallo*.

By 1400 the Venetians had perfected a clear, colorless glass called *cristallo*. The first *cristallo* objects were simple drinking glasses, but technical advances meant that by the mid-16th century the Venetians were producing more delicate forms, including goblets with intricate stems, finely decorated plates, and ornamental ships called nefs.

Venetian glassmakers revived decorative techniques that had been used by the ancient Romans and developed new ones. Among the techniques they revived was *millefiori*, which means "a thousand flowers." This prettily patterned glass was made by fusing

Gonzaga Family

The **Gonzaga were a powerful Italian landowning and military family who seized control of the small city-state of Mantua in 1328. They were to rule the city for the next 300 years. During that time Mantua enjoyed political stability and became a center of culture, attracting many writers, painters, and architects to work there.**

The Gonzaga family rose to power in 1328, when Luigi Gonzaga (1267–1360) deposed the lord of Mantua, who was his brother-in-law Rinaldo Bonacolsi, after a fierce struggle. Luigi's new status as lord of Mantua was legitimized a few years later when he was appointed imperial vicar by the Holy Roman emperor. This meant he was authorized by the emperor to act as his steward over his territory.

TIGHTENING THEIR HOLD

Over the following century the Gonzaga gradually tightened their hold over the city, strengthening its fortifications, constructing many churches, and enhancing Mantua's reputation. Their success as condottieri (mercenary soldiers) for Venice and Milan provided the wealth that allowed them to achieve these things. Like other ruling families of Italy, the Gonzaga

Below: The court of Ludovico III, shown in one of a series of paintings by Andrea Mantegna on the walls of the Camera degli Sposi in the ducal palace in Mantua.

were anxious to safeguard their position by turning it into a hereditary right. Since the title of imperial vicar-

> *The Gonzaga were eager to acquire noble titles such as marquis or duke that could be passed on*

general could not be inherited, the Gonzaga were eager to acquire noble titles such as marquis or duke that could be passed on. Another way the Gonzaga safeguarded their position and wealth was by arranging diplomatic marriages for their children.

In 1432 Luigi's great-grandson Gianfrancesco I (died 1444) was re-

Above: The church of Sant'Andrea, designed by the architect Leon Battista Alberti for Ludovico III.

warded for his services to the Holy Roman emperor Sigismund by being given the title of marquis for himself and his descendants. The same year he reinforced the imperial tie by securing the marriage of his son Ludovico to Sigismund's daughter, Barbara of Brandenburg. These imperial connections helped assure Mantua's independence at a time when many other city-states were losing theirs. Mantua's growing reputation was enough to warrant official visits from Pope Pius II and his court in 1459 and the Holy Roman emperor in the next century.

CITY OF CULTURE

When Gianfrancesco I invited Vittorino da Feltre to Mantua in 1423 to set up a school based on humanist principles, it was the first step toward making Mantua famous throughout Italy. Gianfrancesco's son, Ludovico III (died 1478), was like his father a celebrated soldier and a renowned patron of the arts. Under the patronage of these two enlightened rulers Mantua rapidly became a city of Renaissance culture. The Florentine architect Leon Battista Alberti (1404–1472) was hired to design the magnificent churches of

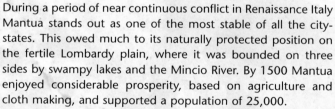

MANTUA

During a period of near continuous conflict in Renaissance Italy Mantua stands out as one of the most stable of all the city-states. This owed much to its naturally protected position on the fertile Lombardy plain, where it was bounded on three sides by swampy lakes and the Mincio River. By 1500 Mantua enjoyed considerable prosperity, based on agriculture and cloth making, and supported a population of 25,000.

Situated halfway between the larger and more powerful city-states of Milan and Venice, Mantua provided a useful buffer zone against their expansion and looked to both for protection. Mantua also owed its stability to the Gonzaga, who established themselves as *signori* (lords) of Mantua in the 14th century. *Signori* were authorized by the emperor or pope to act as vicars (stewards) over their territories, and the Gonzaga were one of the few family regimes in Italy to survive longer than a couple of generations.

From about 1430 Mantua became a center of humanism and the arts thanks to the presence of Vittorino da Feltre's humanist school and people such as the artist Andrea Mantegna, the writer Baldassare Castiglione (1478–1529), and the architect Leon Battista Alberti.

THE FIRST HUMANIST SCHOOL

In 1423 Vittorino da Feltre (1378–1446), a renowned humanist schoolmaster from Padua, was invited to Mantua by Gianfrancesco I to teach his children. Vittorio's school soon earned itself the nickname La Giocosa ("The House of Joy"), and before long it opened its doors to the sons of Mantua's leading families and then (as its reputation spread) to those of rulers and thinkers from across Italy. In the process it gained a reputation as "the first great school of the Renaissance" and helped educate two of Italy's most enlightened Renaissance rulers—Ludovico Gonzaga and Federigo da Montefeltro, duke of Urbino—as well as the humanist Lorenzo Valla.

Vittorino's pupils included middle-aged men as well as the sons of commoners and the nobility. Gifted students from poor backgrounds were taught for free, fulfilling da Feltre's commitment to unlock the talents of all through education. Based on the classical (ancient Greek and Roman) ideas of education, the school taught a broad liberal education. It aimed to encourage the full development of the individual through the study of the classics and a combination of moral and physical instruction.

Subjects taught at the school included Latin, Greek, mathematics (including geometry), science (including astronomy), music and dance, art, and physical education. Rhetoric (the art of persuasive speech or writing) was a key subject, since it provided a useful tool for turning private moral virtue into public political action.

Sant'Andrea and San Sebastiano, and the painter Andrea Mantegna (1431–1506) was invited to become a permanent guest of the Gonzaga court. There he produced one of his greatest works, the *Camera degli Sposi*, a series of frescoes in the "wedding chamber" of the Palazzo Ducale. These paintings showed scenes of Ludovico and members of his family and court arrayed in all their magnificence. Mantegna later produced another series of paintings entitled the *Triumph of Caesar* for Ludovico's son Federigo.

Left: A view of Mantua and the Mincio River from the dome of the church of Sant' Andrea. Many of the fine buildings erected in Mantua in the Renaissance period can still be seen today.

Ludovico's grandson, Francesco II (1466–1519) reigned for over 30 years and was probably the most influential of all the Gonzaga rulers. In the Italian wars that followed the invasion of Italy by the French in 1494 Francesco allied himself with the Holy Roman emperor Charles V. Francesco distinguished himself on the battlefield by leading the allied Italian forces to victory against the French army at the battle of Fornovo. During this period, when northern Italy was beset by turmoil, Mantua was one of the few city-states to retain its independence.

ISABELLA D'ESTE

Francesco's wife was Isabella d'Este, from the dynasty that presided over the small city-state of Ferrara. During this difficult period Isabella ruled Mantua shrewdly in Francesco's absence. A highly accomplished and well-educated woman, Isabella greatly enhanced the reputation of the Gonzaga court by her generous patronage of poetry and drama. Her reputation and her regular correspondence with many of the great

> *During this difficult period Isabella ruled Mantua shrewdly in Francesco's absence*

leaders and thinkers of the time led one cousin to describe her as *la prima donna del mondo* ("the first woman of the world").

Francesco's son, Federigo II (died 1540), was also a great patron of the arts, and during his reign the arts flourished in Mantua as never before. He invited Giulio Romano—a pupil of

the artist Raphael—to carry out work in the city. Romano drained the marshes, restored many villas, and built the impressive Palazzo del Te in the new mannerist style. Many writers and painters also found employment or encouragement in Mantua during this period, including Castiglione and Titian, who painted Federigo's portrait.

DECLINE OF THE GONZAGA

After the Peace of Cambrai (1529) between Charles V and Francis I of France Federigo was promoted to duke of Mantua as reward for his imperial services. When he died in 1540 the house of Gonzaga went into decline. His son Francesco died young, leaving Mantua in the hands of Federigo's brother, Guglielmo. Guglielmo was a spendthrift and a poor ruler, as were his son and grandsons. In the 17th century Mantua was invaded several times and was seized by Austria in 1708.

Above: A portrait of Eleonora Gonzaga, wife of Federigo II, painted by Titian (about 1488–1576). Many painters found employment at Federigo's court.

Gothic Art

The term "Gothic" is used to describe the art that was produced in northern Europe from the end of the 12th century to the middle of the 15th century. It includes everything from architecture, sculpture, and painting to stained glass, manuscript illumination, metalwork, and tapestries. The Gothic style was first seen in the new cathedrals that were built in France, Germany, and England during the late Middle Ages. It flourished in the thriving city of Paris and spread to royal and noble courts across Europe.

Below: A view of the inside of Chartres Cathedral in France, which was largely built between 1194 and 1221. Chartres was one of the earliest and most splendid examples of Gothic architecture.

The 16th-century Italian painter and art historian Giorgio Vasari was the first person to describe medieval art as Gothic, using the term in a negative sense. He rated art produced in the Middle Ages as inferior to that of the classical civilizations of ancient Greece and Rome, and the Italian art of his own time. He saw it as the product of the barbarians, or Goths, who had destroyed the Roman Empire. In dismissing medieval artists as "Gothic," he failed to see that Gothic artists had been part of a great artistic revival.

GOTHIC CATHEDRALS

Cathedrals and churches are the best-known examples of Gothic art. A huge number of cathedrals were built in the prosperous cities of northern Europe from the second half of the 13th century. They were designed to be as tall as possible, soaring up to the heavens to the glory of God. They were also magnificent, with large stained-glass windows and lots of sculpture. Masons (builders skilled in working with stone) developed a new way to build them. They constructed a stone framework consisting of tall, slender columns and pointed arches. Vaulted stone ceilings were made by connecting the arches with stone ribs and filling the gaps between. Stone props called buttresses were built around the outside of the cathedral to stabilize the structure. Because this stone framework supported the weight of the cathedral, massive stone walls were not needed, so there was plenty of space for large windows.

Below: **The Virgin and Child,** *a silver statue covered in gold made in about 1324–1339 in Paris. As well as carving in stone, Gothic sculptors excelled at making small, carefully crafted statues from precious metals.*

As more cathedrals were built, the Gothic style became more and more elaborate. In France a style called the rayonnant developed. It was named after the "radiating" pattern of the tracery (stone bars) that supported the pieces of glass in the huge round windows—called "rose" windows—that were popular in cathedrals. All over Europe masons used elegant patterns of stone tracery to decorate walls and ceilings as well as windows. In Spain the Gothic style became so intricate and elaborate that it was later called plateresque, which literally means "like silversmith's work."

SCULPTURE

Sculpture played an important part in Gothic cathedrals. Carved figures were used to decorate the west front (where the main entrance was sited) and to adorn altarpieces, screens, and the tops of columns, as well as tombs. Although these sculptures look stiff today, they were lighter and more elegant than earlier carvings had been. Typical Gothic figure sculptures are tall, with elongated proportions, and have long robes gathered into deeply carved folds. Gothic sculptors delighted in the patterns created by folds in clothes and long wavy beards and tresses of hair.

Color was an important part of Gothic art, and many sculptures were painted and gilded (covered in gold). Because so much wall space was given over to stained glass windows, there was less room for wall paintings than in earlier times. However, the windows themselves were great pieces of art.

STAINED GLASS AND PICTURES

The glass used to make windows was painted and stained in jewellike colors to show pictures of holy figures and Bible stories. Pictures were also painted on wooden panels to stand behind altars. However, in northern Europe some of the greatest examples of Gothic painting appeared in illuminated (illustrated) manuscripts such as Bibles and prayer books. The characteristics of Gothic painting are similar to those of sculpture: elongated proportions, graceful poses, patterns of long folds in clothes, and stylized (artificial looking) faces. Gothic artists loved to use expensive materials such as gold, which was often made into the background of a picture and halos of light around the heads of holy people.

LESSONS IN STONE AND PAINT

In the medieval period sculptures and paintings were intended to instruct people—most of whom could neither read nor write—in the lessons of Christianity. They brought to life the priests' sermons and so had to be easy to understand. Each holy figure was depicted in a set way so that they were easily recognizable. Artists either copied other pictures or used books called pattern or model books that were like visual encyclopedias, showing all the subjects they were likely to need. Gothic paintings and sculptures were stylized because that is what people expected to see. Gothic artists were quite capable of copying nature when they wanted to. Intricately carved

Left: **The Adoration of the Magi** *(1423)* *by Gentile da Fabriano, which shows the three kings worshiping the baby Jesus. The lavish use of gold, rich colors, and detailed depiction of sumptuous fabrics are typical of the highly decorative International Gothic style.*

leaves at the tops of columns and carefully observed plants in paintings and tapestries are all characteristics of Gothic art. Some artists also became interested in depicting humans in a lifelike way. But holy figures and Bible stories were seen as separate from nature and so were portrayed in different ways.

INTERNATIONAL GOTHIC

Although Gothic art is most closely associated with cathedrals, it also became popular with secular (non-religious) patrons. Most earlier artists had worked in monasteries, but during the medieval period an increasing number of artists set up workshops in cities around royal and noble courts. An important cultural center in the 13th and 14th centuries was Paris, where the French king Louis IX had a flourishing court. Secular patrons like Louis encouraged artists to develop the elaborate, graceful, and luxurious qualities of Gothic art. A highly refined style of courtly art developed and spread through Europe toward the end of the 14th century. This style is often called the "International Gothic." Courts in Burgundy, Prague, and northern Italy became important centers of this style, and sumptuous paintings by Italian artists such as Gentile da Fabriano are magnificent examples of its splendor.

SEE ALSO
- Architecture
- Glass
- Painting
- Religious Themes in Art
- Sculpture
- Tombs and Monuments
- Vasari

Government, Systems of

During the Renaissance there were great changes in the way that people were governed. In most western European countries centralized forms of government began to replace the more fragmented power structures of the Middle Ages, when most people were subject to local lords. In some regions cities became self-governing and were practically independent of their overlords.

During the medieval period most of the people of western Europe owed allegiance to a local lord and military leader. In theory the lords also owed allegiance to an overlord, usually a king, but in practice they were largely independent and fought among each other for power. Only periodically did a king become strong enough to control his lords for any length of time.

There was little of the centralized administration that we associate with government today. There was no permanent bureaucracy (body of government officers), no centralized system of paying taxes, no permanent army, and no widely accepted legal codes. Justice was administered locally on the basis of traditional rights, duties, and privileges. Only the church kept alive the ancient Roman idea of government, with a bureaucracy of educated men and a system of courts administering church law.

Left: A detail from a 14th-century wall painting in Siena town hall, Italy, entitled Good Government. *The picture shows the harmonious relationship between a town and the countryside around it, as nobles and merchants pass through fields tended by peasants.*

Left: A 16th-century gold plaque showing the French king Francis I holding court. Francis was one of the strongest kings of the Renaissance and kept the power of the local lords firmly in check.

Toward the end of the medieval period some kings became powerful enough to exert their authority over local lords and impose a unified rule over their lands. These strong kings generally ruled with the help of a council of ministers, a system of government known as monarchy.

STRENGTHENING THE MONARCHY

One way monarchs strengthened their power over their lords was by encouraging them to spend time at court in the hope of winning an important place in the government. Monarchical government developed in France, England, and Spain, and went hand in hand with the development of large, unified states. The people of such states were no longer vassals to local lords but subjects of a national monarch.

Francis I of France (ruled 1515–1547) was one king who was especially determined to assert his authority over his whole kingdom. He doubled taxes, increased the number of royal officers, and ignored the traditional rights and privileges of local communities. He also visited as many parts of France as he could, showing himself to his people, most of whom had never seen their king before.

Many French thinkers of the time supported the idea of an all-powerful, or absolute, monarch. However, even the most powerful king could not rule without the cooperation of his subjects. Because Renaissance kings could not afford to keep a large permanent army, they could not enforce their rule by military means. When they needed an army, kings remained dependent on local lords and their men.

One way the king could gain the cooperation of his subjects was through patronage—granting favors and gifts to those who helped him carry out his rule. Another way was by consulting and working with assemblies that represented his subjects' interests. In France, for example, the king ruled with the help of a state assembly known as the Estates-General. This assembly was made up of elected representatives from the three "estates"—the clergy, the nobility, and the wealthy inhabitants of towns and cities. In England the Tudor monarchs often worked closely with Parliament, which was roughly the equivalent of the French Estates-General.

The deep flaw in monarchical government was that it depended on the abilities of a single man or woman. A weak monarch could plunge a country into disaster. The lack of an obvious or suitable heir could lead to civil war and the breakdown of government into a state of anarchy (no rule at all). This happened in France after 1559, when the sudden death of Henry II (ruled 1547–1559) meant that power passed into the hands of Henry's wife, Catherine de Medici (1519–1589), who proved unable to control the rival factions that fought for power.

CITY-STATES

In the late Middle Ages towns and cities increased in size and prosperity. They became major centers of trade, and many became wealthy enough to buy their freedom from local overlords. These prosperous cities became self-ruling and formed communal

THE ENGLISH PARLIAMENT

First set up in the 13th century, the English Parliament was a state assembly summoned by the king to give advice and assent to his laws. It comprised representatives of lords, clergy, knights, and citizens from all over the country. Under the Tudor monarchs Parliament became much more powerful and took on a legislative, or law-making, role. It first assumed greater importance when King Henry VIII enlisted the support of its members to create a national church free from papal control—so that he could divorce his first wife Catherine of Aragon. From this time onward Parliament met more regularly than it had before and became a more important instrument in

government. In theory the monarch could make laws by issuing royal proclamations, but in fact rarely did so. Parliament debated the issues of the day and made draft laws, or bills. The monarch had to agree to the bills for them to become actual laws, or acts of Parliament. People who were eligible to vote for the Commons (that is, the people in the Parliament representing citizens and knights) had to own property worth at least 40 shillings, a substantial amount of money in Renaissance England.

Left: The Tudor queen Elizabeth I presiding over Parliament in the Palace of Westminster, London.

governments made up of officers elected by an assembly of the city's male elite. This elite included local landowners, merchants, property owners, and clergy. Women, however, could neither vote nor hold office.

To administer their growing cities, the communes developed new political institutions, which were often based in a town hall built overlooking the city's main square. They developed bureaucracies to run city affairs, such as looking after roads and bridges, overseeing the craft guilds, and raising

Communes developed new political institutions to run their growing cities

armies in times of trouble. The communes also set up civic constitutions, which stated exactly who could hold office and for how long. In Florence, for instance, the nine members of the main governing body, called the *signoria,* could only hold office for two months. Such measures were intended to ensure that no individual or faction could acquire too much power.

By the 14th century, however, many communal governments had fallen into the hands of a few wealthy families. In Brussels, for example, a few merchant families controlled not only business and civic affairs but also the law courts. In some Italian cities a single leader, called a *signore,* took control—sometimes by force of arms—and in some cases was able to ensure that his rule became hereditary. Such ruling families, including the Visconti of Milan and the Montefeltro

of Urbino, often acquired noble titles such as duke or marquis and ruled their territories as virtual monarchs.

A few cities clung to the old communal traditions, including the republics of Venice, Lucca, Siena, and for a time, Florence, although all in fact were strongly oligarchic—that is, they were ruled by a small group of people. Venice was widely admired for its well-ordered government. By the time of the Renaissance Venice had several governing bodies, including the Great Council, the Senate, and the Council of Ten, each of which kept a careful check on the power of the others. The elected Venetian head of state, called the doge, served for life. Although the doge had little real power, he was important as a symbolic figure who helped hold the community together.

Above: A 16th-century painting of the doge of Venice receiving a ring from a fisherman in an ancient ceremony based on a legend.

SEE ALSO
♦ City-States
♦ England
♦ Florence
♦ France
♦ Francis I
♦ Free Cities
♦ Venice

Timeline

♦ **1305** Giotto begins work on frescoes for the Arena Chapel, Padua—he is often considered the father of Renaissance art.

♦ **1321** Dante publishes the *Divine Comedy*, which has a great influence on later writers.

♦ **1327** Petrarch begins writing the sonnets known as the *Canzoniere*.

♦ **1337** The start of the Hundred Years' War between England and France.

♦ **1353** Boccaccio writes the *Decameron*, an influential collection of 100 short stories.

♦ **1368** The Ming dynasty comes to power in China.

♦ **1377** Pope Gregory XI moves the papacy back to Rome from Avignon, where it has been based since 1309.

♦ **1378** The Great Schism begins: two popes, Urban VI and Clement VII, both lay claim to the papacy.

♦ **1378** English theologian John Wycliffe criticizes the practices of the Roman Catholic church.

♦ **1380** Ivan I of Muscovy defeats the army of the Mongol Golden Horde at the battle of Kulikovo.

♦ **1389** The Ottomans defeat the Serbs at the battle of Kosovo, beginning a new phase of Ottoman expansion.

♦ **1397** Sigismund of Hungary is defeated by the Ottoman Turks at the battle of Nicopolis.

♦ **1397** Queen Margaret of Denmark unites Denmark, Sweden, and Norway under the Union of Kalmar.

♦ **1398** The Mongol leader Tamerlane invades India.

♦ **1399** Henry Bolingbroke becomes Henry IV of England.

♦ **1400** English writer Geoffrey Chaucer dies, leaving his *Canterbury Tales* unfinished.

♦ **1403** In Italy the sculptor Ghiberti wins a competition to design a new set of bronze doors for Florence Cathedral.

♦ **c.1402** The Bohemian preacher Jan Hus begins to attack the corruption of the church.

♦ **1405** The Chinese admiral Cheng Ho commands the first of seven expeditions to the Indian Ocean and East Africa.

♦ **1415** Jan Hus is summoned to the Council of Constance and condemned to death.

♦ **1415** Henry V leads the English to victory against the French at the battle of Agincourt.

♦ **c.1415** Florentine sculptor Donatello produces his sculpture *Saint George*.

♦ **1416** Venice defeats the Ottoman fleet at the battle of Gallipoli, but does not check the Ottoman advance.

♦ **1417** The Council of Constance elects Martin V pope, ending the Great Schism.

♦ **1418** Brunelleschi designs the dome of Florence Cathedral.

♦ **1420** Pope Martin V returns the papacy to Rome, bringing peace and order to the city.

♦ **c.1420** Prince Henry of Portugal founds a school of navigation at Sagres, beginning a great age of Portuguese exploration.

♦ **1422** Charles VI of France dies, leaving his throne to the English king Henry VI. Charles VI's son also claims the throne.

♦ **c.1425** Florentine artist Masaccio paints the *Holy Trinity*, the first painting to use the new science of perspective.

♦ **1429** Joan of Arc leads the French to victory at Orléans; Charles VII is crowned king of France in Reims Cathedral.

♦ **1431** The English burn Joan of Arc at the stake for heresy.

♦ **1433** Sigismund of Luxembourg becomes Holy Roman emperor.

♦ **1434** Cosimo de Medici comes to power in Florence.

♦ **1434** The Flemish artist Jan van Eyck paints the *Arnolfini Marriage* using the newly developed medium of oil paint.

♦ **1439** The Council of Florence proclaims the reunion of the Western and Orthodox churches.

♦ **c.1440** Donatello completes his statue of David—the first life-size bronze sculpture since antiquity.

♦ **1443** Federigo da Montefeltro becomes ruler of Urbino.

♦ **1447** The Milanese people declare their city a republic.

♦ **1450** The condottiere Francesco Sforza seizes control of Milan.

♦ **1450** Fra Angelico paints *The Annunciation* for the monastery of San Marco in Florence.

♦ **1453** Constantinople, capital of the Byzantine Empire, falls to the Ottomans and becomes the capital of the Muslim Empire.

♦ **1453** The French defeat the English at the battle of Castillon, ending the Hundred Years' War.

♦ **1454–1456** Venice, Milan, Florence, Naples, and the papacy form the Italian League to maintain peace in Italy.

♦ **1455** The start of the Wars of the Roses between the Houses of York and Lancaster in England.

♦ **c.1455** The German Johannes Gutenberg develops the first printing press using movable type.

♦ **1456** The Florentine painter Uccello begins work on the *Battle of San Romano*.

♦ **1461** The House of York wins the Wars of the Roses; Edward IV becomes king of England.

♦ **1461** Sonni Ali becomes king of the Songhai Empire in Africa.

♦ **1462** Marsilio Ficino founds the Platonic Academy of Florence— the birthplace of Renaissance Neoplatonism.

♦ **1463** War breaks out between Venice and the Ottoman Empire.

♦ **1465** The Italian painter Mantegna begins work on the Camera degli Sposi in Mantua.

♦ **1467** Civil war breaks out in Japan, lasting for over a century.

♦ **1469** Lorenzo the Magnificent, grandson of Cosimo de Medici, comes to power in Florence.

♦ **1469** The marriage of Isabella I of Castile and Ferdinand V of Aragon unites the two kingdoms.

♦ **1470** The Florentine sculptor Verrocchio completes his *David*.

♦ **1476** William Caxton establishes the first English printing press at Westminster, near London.

♦ **1477** Pope Sixtus IV begins building the Sistine Chapel.

♦ **c.1477** Florentine painter Sandro Botticelli paints the *Primavera*, one of the first large-scale mythological paintings of the Renaissance.

♦ **1478** The Spanish Inquisition is founded in Spain.

♦ **1480** The Ottoman fleet destroys the port of Otranto in south Italy.

♦ **1485** Henry Tudor becomes Henry VII of England—the start of the Tudor dynasty.

♦ **1486** *The Witches' Hammer* is published, a handbook on how to hunt down witches.

♦ **1488** Portuguese navigator Bartholomeu Dias reaches the Cape of Good Hope.

♦ **1491** Missionaries convert King Nzina Nkowu of the Congo to Christianity.

♦ **1492** The Spanish monarchs conquer Granada, the last Moorish territory in Spain.

♦ **1492** Christopher Columbus lands in the Bahamas, claiming the territory for Spain.

♦ **1492** Henry VII of England renounces all English claims to the French throne.

♦ **1493** The Hapsburg Maximilian becomes Holy Roman emperor.

♦ **1494** Charles VIII of France invades Italy, beginning four decades of Italian wars.

♦ **1494** In Italy Savonarola comes to power in Florence.

♦ **1494** The Treaty of Tordesillas divides the non-Christian world between Spain and Portugal.

♦ **1495** Leonardo da Vinci begins work on *The Last Supper* .

♦ **1495** Spain forms a Holy League with the Holy Roman emperor and expels the French from Naples.

♦ **1498** Portuguese navigator Vasco da Gama reaches Calicut, India.

♦ **1498** German artist Dürer creates the *Apocalypse* woodcuts.

♦ **1500** Portuguese navigator Pedro Cabral discovers Brazil.

♦ **c.1500–1510** Dutch painter Hieronymous Bosch paints *The Garden of Earthly Delights*.

♦ **c.1502** Italian architect Donato Bramante designs the Tempietto Church in Rome.

♦ **1503** Leonardo da Vinci begins painting the *Mona Lisa*.

♦ **1504** Michelangelo finishes his statue of David, widely seen as a symbol of Florence.

♦ **c.1505** Venetian artist Giorgione paints *The Tempest*.

♦ **1506** The Italian architect Donato Bramante begins work on rebuilding Saint Peter's, Rome.

♦ **1508** Michelangelo begins work on the ceiling of the Sistine Chapel in the Vatican.

♦ **1509** Henry VIII ascends the throne of England.

♦ **1509** The League of Cambrai defeats Venice at the battle of Agnadello.

♦ **1510–1511** Raphael paints *The School of Athens* in the Vatican.

♦ **1511** The French are defeated at the battle of Ravenna in Italy and are forced to retreat over the Alps.

♦ **1513** Giovanni de Medici becomes Pope Leo X.

♦ **1515** Thomas Wolsey becomes lord chancellor of England.

♦ **1515** Francis I becomes king of France. He invades Italy and captures Milan.

♦ **c.1515** German artist Grünewald paints the *Isenheim Altarpiece*.

♦ **1516** Charles, grandson of the emperor Maximilian I, inherits the Spanish throne as Charles I.

♦ **1516** Thomas More publishes his political satire *Utopia*.

♦ **1516** Dutch humanist Erasmus publishes a more accurate version of the Greek New Testament.

♦ **1517** Martin Luther pins his 95 theses on the door of the castle church in Wittenburg.

♦ **1519** Charles I of Spain becomes Holy Roman emperor Charles V.

♦ **1519–1521** Hernán Cortés conquers Mexico for Spain.

♦ **1520** Henry VIII of England and Francis I of France meet at the Field of the Cloth of Gold to sign a treaty of friendship.

♦ **1520** Portuguese navigator Ferdinand Magellan discovers a route to the Indies around the tip of South America.

♦ **1520** Süleyman the Magnificent becomes ruler of the Ottoman Empire, which now dominates the eastern Mediterranean.

♦ **1520–1523** Titian paints *Bacchus and Ariadne* for Alfonso d'Este.

♦ **1521** Pope Leo X excommuicates Martin Luther.

♦ **1521** The emperor Charles V attacks France, beginning a long period of European war.

♦ **1522** Ferdinand Magellan's ship the *Victoria* is the first to sail around the world.

♦ **1523–1525** Huldrych Zwingli sets up a Protestant church at Zurich in Switzerland.

♦ **1525** In Germany the Peasants' Revolt is crushed, and its leader, Thomas Münzer, is executed.

♦ **1525** The emperor Charles V defeats the French at the battle of Pavia and takes Francis I prisoner.

♦ **1525** William Tyndale translates the New Testament into English.

♦ **1526** The Ottoman Süleyman the Magnificent defeats Hungary at the battle of Mohács.

♦ **1526** Muslim Mongol leader Babur invades northern India and establishes the Mogul Empire.

♦ **c.1526** The Italian artist Correggio paints the *Assumption of the Virgin* in Parma Cathedral.

♦ **1527** Charles V's armies overrun Italy and sack Rome.

♦ **1527–1530** Gustavus I founds a Lutheran state church in Sweden.

♦ **1528** Italian poet and humanist Baldassare Castiglione publishes *The Courtier*.

♦ **1529** The Ottoman Süleyman the Magnificent lays siege to Vienna, but eventually retreats.

♦ **1530** The Catholic church issues the "Confutation," attacking Luther and Protestantism.

♦ **1531** The Protestant princes of Germany form the Schmalkaldic League.

♦ **1531–1532** Francisco Pizarro conquers Peru for Spain.

♦ **1532** Machiavelli's *The Prince* is published after his death.

♦ **1533** Henry VIII of England rejects the authority of the pope and marries Anne Boleyn.

♦ **1533** Anabaptists take over the city of Münster in Germany.

♦ **1533** Christian III of Denmark founds the Lutheran church of Denmark.

♦ **1534** Paul III becomes pope and encourages the growth of new religious orders such as the Jesuits.

♦ **1534** Luther publishes his German translation of the Bible.

♦ **1534** The Act of Supremacy declares Henry VIII supreme head of the Church of England.

♦ **c.1535** Parmigianino paints the mannerist masterpiece *Madonna of the Long Neck*.

♦ **1535–1536** The Swiss city of Geneva becomes Protestant and expels the Catholic clergy.

♦ **1536** Calvin publishes *Institutes of the Christian Religion*, which sets out his idea of predestination.

♦ **1536** Pope Paul III sets up a reform commission to examine the state of the Catholic church.

♦ **1537** Hans Holbein is appointed court painter to Henry VIII of England.

♦ **1539** Italian painter Bronzino begins working for Cosimo de Medici the Younger in Florence.

♦ **1539** Ignatius de Loyola founds the Society of Jesus (the Jesuits).

♦ **1541** John Calvin sets up a model Christian city in Geneva.

♦ **1543** Andreas Vesalius publishes *On the Structure of the Human Body*, a handbook of anatomy based on dissections.

♦ **1543** Polish astronomer Copernicus's *On the Revolutions of the Heavenly Spheres* proposes a sun-centered universe.

♦ **1544** Charles V and Francis I of France sign the Truce of Crespy.

♦ **1545** Pope Paul III organizes the Council of Trent to counter the threat of Protestantism.

♦ **1545** Spanish explorers find huge deposits of silver in the Andes Mountains of Peru.

♦ **1547** Charles V defeats the Protestant Schmalkaldic League at the Battle of Mühlberg.

♦ **1547** Ivan IV "the Terrible" declares himself czar of Russia.

♦ **1548** Titian paints the equestrian portrait *Charles V after the Battle of Mühlberg*.

♦ **1548** Tintoretto paints *Saint Mark Rescuing the Slave*.

♦ **1550** Italian Georgio Vasari publishes his *Lives of the Artists*.

♦ **1553** Mary I of England restores the Catholic church.

♦ **1554** Work begins on the Cathedral of Saint Basil in Red Square, Moscow.

♦ **1555** At the Peace of Augsburg Charles V allows the German princes to determine their subjects' religion.

♦ **1556** Ivan IV defeats the last Mongol khanates. Muscovy now dominates the Volga region.

♦ **1556** Philip II becomes king of Spain.

♦ **1559** Elizabeth I of England restores the Protestant church.

♦ **1562** The Wars of Religion break out in France.

♦ **1565** Flemish artist Pieter Bruegel the Elder paints *Hunters in the Snow*.

♦ **1565** Italian architect Palladio designs the Villa Rotunda, near Vicenza.

♦ **1566** The Dutch revolt against the Spanish over the loss of political and religious freedoms:

Philip II of Spain sends 10,000 troops under the duke of Alba to suppress the revolt.

♦ **1569** Flemish cartographer Mercator produces a world map using a new projection.

♦ **1571** Philip II of Spain and an allied European force defeat the Ottomans at the battle of Lepanto.

♦ **1572** In Paris, France, a Catholic mob murders thousands of Huguenots in the Saint Bartholomew's Day Massacre.

♦ **1572** Danish astronomer Tycho Brahe sees a new star.

♦ **1573** Venetian artist Veronese paints the *Feast of the House of Levi*.

♦ **1579** The seven northern provinces of the Netherlands form the Union of Utrecht.

♦ **1580** Giambologna creates his mannerist masterpiece *Flying Mercury*.

♦ **1585** Henry III of France bans Protestantism in France; civil war breaks out again in the War of the Three Henrys.

♦ **1586** El Greco, a Greek artist active in Spain, paints the *Burial of Count Orgaz*.

♦ **1587** Mary, Queen of Scots, is executed by Elizabeth I of England.

♦ **c.1587** Nicholas Hilliard paints the miniature *Young Man among Roses*.

♦ **1588** Philip II of Spain launches his great Armada against England —but the fleet is destroyed.

♦ **1589** Henry of Navarre becomes king of France as Henry IV.

♦ **1592–1594** Tintoretto paints *The Last Supper*.

♦ **1596** Edmund Spencer publishes the *Faerie Queene*, glorifying Elizabeth I as "Gloriana."

♦ **1598** Henry IV of France grants Huguenots and Catholics equal political rights.

♦ **1598** In England the Globe Theater is built on London's south bank; it stages many of Shakespeare's plays.

♦ **1600–1601** Caravaggio paints *The Crucifixion of Saint Peter*, an early masterpiece of baroque art.

♦ **1603** Elizabeth I of England dies and is succeeded by James I, son of Mary, Queen of Scots.

♦ **1610** Galileo's *The Starry Messenger* supports the sun-centered model of the universe.

♦ **1620** The Italian painter Artemisia Gentileschi paints *Judith and Holofernes*.

Glossary

A.D. The letters A.D. stand for the Latin Anno Domini, which means "in the year of our Lord." Dates with these letters written after them are measured forward from the year Christ was born.

Altarpiece A painting or sculpture placed behind an altar in a church.

Amphitheater A large circular or oval building, often open to the sky, with tiers of seats ranged around a central space. Amphitheaters were used in ancient Rome for spectacles such as games or gladiatorial contests.

Apprentice Someone legally bound to a craftsman for a number of years in order to learn a craft.

Baptistery Part of a church, or a separate building, where people are baptized.

B.C. Short for "Before Christ." Dates with these letters after them are measured backward from the year of Christ's birth.

Bureaucracy A system of government that relies on a body of officials and usually involves much paperwork and many regulations.

Cardinal An official of the Catholic church, highest in rank below the pope. The cardinals elect the pope.

Classical A term used to describe the civilizations of ancient Greece and Rome, and any later art and architecture based on ancient Greek and Roman examples.

Colonnade A row of columns supporting an arched or a flat structure.

Commission An order for a specially made object, like a painting or tapestry.

Condottiere A mercenary soldier, that is, a soldier who will fight for any employer in return for money.

Contemporary Someone or something that lives or exists at the same period of time.

Diet A general assembly of representatives of the Holy Roman Empire.

Flemish A word used to describe someone or something from Flanders, a region including present-day Belgium and parts of the Netherlands and France.

Fresco A type of painting that is usually used for decorating walls and ceilings in which pigments (colors) are painted into wet plaster.

Grotto An artificial cavern, often decorated with fountains and pictures made from shells and stones. Grottoes were popular garden features in ancient Greek and Roman times, and were revived in the Renaissance.

Guild An association of merchants or craftsmen, organized to protect the interests of their members and to regulate the quality of their goods and services.

Hanseatic League A trading association of towns around the Baltic Sea that was set up in the late 13th century. It flourished between the 14th and 16th centuries.

Heresy A belief that is contrary to the accepted teachings of the church.

Heretic Someone whose beliefs contradict those of the church.

Humanism A new way of thinking about human life that characterized the Renaissance. It was based on the study of "humanities"—that is, ancient Greek and Roman texts, history, and philosophy—and stressed the importance of developing rounded, cultured people.

Humanist Someone who adopted humanism, the new way of thinking about human life that characterized the Renaissance.

Hundred Years' War A long-drawn-out war between France and England, lasting from 1337 to 1453. It consisted of a series of campaigns with periods of tense peace in between.

Journeyman A qualified craftsman who has completed his apprenticeship and works for another person on either a specific project or a daily basis.

Laity or lay people Anyone who is not of the clergy.

Majolica A type of pottery made in Spain. It is covered with a white glaze and decorated with brightly colored patterns and scenes.

Mercenary A soldier who will fight for any employer in return for money.

Moat A wide, water-filled ditch that is dug around a fortified building or town for defensive purposes.

Patron Someone who orders and pays for a work of art.

Patronage The act of ordering and paying for a work of art.

Pavilion An ornamental building, often used as a pleasure house; or a decorative feature that is part of a larger building, sometimes with a domed roof.

Perspective A technique that allows artists to create the impression of three-dimensional space in their pictures. Near objects are made to appear larger, and distant objects are shown as smaller.

Piecework Work that is paid for according to the amount done (rather than according to the time it has taken).

Proportions The size and measurements of the different parts of an object and their relationship to one another.

Tempera A type of paint made by mixing pigments (colors) with egg yolk. It was widely used in the Middle Ages and Renaissance.

Theologian Someone who makes a study of religion.

Treatise A book or long essay about the principles, or rules, of a particular subject.

Triptych A picture or carving consisting of three panels side by side. It was often used as an altarpiece.

Vassal A person who is bound to a local lord to whom they owe their loyalty and services.

Vernacular The language of the ordinary people, rather than Latin.

Further Reading

Avery, Charles. *Giambologna: The Complete Sculpture.* New York: Phaidon Press, 1994.

Baumgartner, Frederic J. *France in the Sixteenth Century.* New York: St. Martin's Press, 1995.

Baxandall, Michael. *Limewood Sculptors of Renaissance Germany.* New Haven, CT: Yale University Press, 1982.

Brucker, Gene A. *Florence: The Golden Age 1138–1737.* Berkeley, CA: University of California Press, 1998.

Campbell, W. John. *Hieronymus Bosch.* New York: Harry N. Abrams, 2001.

Chastel, André. *French Art: The Renaissance 1430–1620.* New York: Flammarion, 1995.

Christiansen, Keith, and Judith Mann. *Orazio and Artemisia Gentileschi.* New York: Metropolitan Museum of Art, 2001.

Christiansen, Keith. *Andrea Mantegna: Padua and Mantua.* New York: George Braziller, 1994.

Cloulas, Ivan, and Michèle Bimbenet-Privat. *Treasures of the French Renaissance.* New York: Harry N. Abrams, 1998.

Comito, Terry. *The Idea of the Garden in the Renaissance.* New Brunswick, NJ: Rutgers University Press, 1978.

Cottret, Bernard. *Calvin: A Biography.* Edinburgh, UK: T & T Clark, 2000.

Dunkerton, Jill, Susan Foister, Dillian Gordon, and Nicholas Penny. *Giotto to Dürer: Early Renaissance Painting in the National Gallery.* London: National Gallery Publications, 1991.

Epstein, Steven A. *Genoa and the Genoese, 958–1528.* Chapel Hill, NC: University of North Carolina Press, 2001.

Faggin, Giorgio T. *The Complete Paintings of the Van Eycks.* London: Weidenfeld & Nicolson, 1970.

Friedrichs, Christopher R. *The Early Modern City, 1450–1750.* Reading, MA: Addison-Wesley Publishing, 1995.

Hand, John Oliver, and Martha Wolff. *Early Netherlandish Painting.* Washington, DC: National Gallery of Art, 1986.

Hernàndez, Xavier, and Jordi Ballonga. *Lebek: A City of Northern Europe through the Ages.* Boston, MA: Houghton Mifflin, 1991.

Hibbert, Christopher. *The House of Medici: Its Rise and Fall.* New York: Quill, 1999.

Hills, Paul. *Venetian Color: Marble, Mosaic, Painting and Glass 1250–1550.* New

Haven, CT: Yale University Press, 1999.

Kent, Dale. *Cosimo de'Medici and the Florentine Renaissance.* New Haven, CT: Yale University Press, 2000.

Knecht, R. J. *Francis I.* Cambridge, UK: Cambridge University Press, 1982.

Knecht, R. J. *French Renaissance Monarchy: Francis I and Henry II.* London: Longman, 1996.

Knecht, R.J. *The Rise and Fall of Renaissance France, 1483–1610.* Oxford: Blackwell Publishers, 2001.

Koldeweij, Jos, Paul Vandenbroeck, and Bernard Vermet. *Hieronymus Bosch: The Complete Paintings and Drawings.* New York: Harry N. Abrams, 2001.

Krautheimer, Richard. *Lorenzo Ghiberti.* Princeton, NJ: Princeton University Press, 1982.

Martindale, Andrew. *Gothic Art.* London: Thames & Hudson, 1985.

Monter, E. William. *Calvin's Geneva.* New York: Wiley, 1967.

Mueller, Anne. *Giotto.* Cologne, Germany: Könemann, 1998.

Oggins, Robin S. *Castles and Fortresses.* New York: Metrobooks, 1995.

Orenstein, Nadine M. *Pieter Bruegel the Elder: Prints and Drawings.* New Haven, CT: Yale University Press, 2001.

Philip, Lotte Brand. *The Ghent Altarpiece and the Art of Jan van Eyck.* Princeton, NJ: Princeton University Press, 1971.

Pignatti, Terisio, and Filippo Pedrocco. *Giorgione.* New York: Rizzoli, 1999.

Pozzoli, Milena Ercole. *Castles of the Loire.* New York: Stewart, Tabori & Chang, 1997.

Puyvelde, Leo van. *Flemish Painting from the Van Eycks to Metsys.* London: Weidenfeld & Nicolson, 1971.

Reston, Jr., James. *Galileo: A Life.* New York: HarperCollins Publishers, 1994.

Roeder, Ralph. *The Man of the Renaissance: Four Lawgivers, Savonarola, Machiavelli, Castiglione, Aretino.* Clifton, NJ: A. M. Kelley, 1977.

Seward, Desmond. *Prince of the Renaissance; the Golden Life of François I.* New York: Macmillan, 1973.

Shepherd, J.C. *Italian Gardens of the Renaissance.* Princeton, NJ: Princeton Architectural Press, 1993.

Simon, Kate. *A Renaissance Tapestry.* New York: Harper & Row, 1988.

Sís, Peter. *Starry Messenger.* New York: Farrar, Straus & Giroux, 1996.

Stubblebine, James H. *Giotto: The Arena Chapel Frescoes.* New York: W.W. Norton, 1996.

Venezia, Mike. *Giotto.* New York: Children's Press, 2000.

White, Michael. *Galileo Galilei: Inventor, Astronomer, and Rebel.* Woodbridge, CT: Blackbirch Press, 1999.

Wilson, Peter H. *The Holy Roman Empire, 1495–1806.* New York: St. Martin's Press, 1999.

Zelasco, Marco. *Florence in the 1400s.* Austin, TX: Raintree/Steck Vaughn, 2001.

Zerner, Henri. *The School of Fontainebleau: Etchings and Engravings.* London: Thames & Hudson, 1969.

Ziermann, Horst. *Matthias Grünewald.* New York: Prestel, 2001.

Zuffi, Stefano. *Dürer: Master Draftsman of the Renaissance—His Life in Paintings.* New York: DK Publishing, 1999.

WEBSITES

World history site
www.historyworld.net

BBC Online: History
www.bbc.co.uk/history

The Webmuseum's tour of the Renaissance
www.oir.ucf.edu/wm/paint/glo/renaissance/

Virtual time travel tour of the Renaissance
library.thinkquest.org/3588/Renaissance/

The Renaissance
www.learner.org/exhibits/renaissance

National Gallery of Art—tour of 16th-century Italian paintings
www.nga.gov/collection/gallery/ita16.htm

Uffizi Art Gallery, Florence
musa.uffizi.firenze.it/welcomeE.html

Database of Renaissance artists
www.artcyclopedia.com/index.html

Set Index

Picture Credits

MAPS
The maps in this book show the locations of cities, states, and empires of the
Renaissance period. However, for the sake of clarity, present-day place names are
often used.